# The Labor Market:
# An Information System

# Boris Yavitz
# Dean W. Morse
## with
# Anna B. Dutka
foreword by
Eli Ginzberg

Conservation of Human Resources Studies—
Columbia University

# The Labor Market: An Information System

PRAEGER SPECIAL STUDIES IN U.S. ECONOMIC, SOCIAL, AND POLITICAL ISSUES

**Praeger Publishers**    New York    Washington    London

Library of Congress Cataloging in Publication Data

Yavitz, Boris
    The labor market.

    (Conservation of human resources series)
(Praeger special studies in U. S. economic, social,
and political issues)
    1. Labor supply.   I.  Morse, Dean, joint
author.   II.  Title.   III.  Series.
HD5707. Y38          331. 1'1          73-25

PRAEGER PUBLISHERS
111 Fourth Avenue, New York, N.Y. 10003, U.S.A.
5, Cromwell Place, London S.W.7, England

Published in the United States of America in 1973
by Praeger Publishers, Inc.

Printed in the United States of America

This report was prepared for the Manpower Administration, U.S.
Department of Labor, under research number 70-34-70-04
authorized by Title I of the Manpower Development and Training
Act. Since contractors performing research under government
sponsorship are encouraged to express their own judgment freely,
the report does not necessarily represent the department's official
opinion or policy. Moreover, the contractor is solely responsible
for the factual accuracy of all material developed in the report.

The Conservation of Human Resources Project, Columbia University, is an interdisciplinary research group now in its fourth decade of working in the field of human resources and manpower. Its investigations cover a broad spectrum with primary emphasis on the role of human resources in the economic development of the United States but including also other advanced economies and the developing world. In recent years the Conservation Project has increasingly focused on metropolitan labor markets. The Project also engages in research in health policy issues. Professor Eli Ginzberg, 525 Uris, Columbia University, New York, New York 10027, is director of the Project.

This foreword has several objectives. First, we will explain how a group of manpower researchers undertook an assignment to formulate the conceptual foundations of a labor market information system and the manner in which they went about fulfilling this task. Second, we will sketch the changes in the political, technological, and economic environment that placed the issue of a labor market information system on the congressional agenda and that eventually led to favorable action by legislators who earlier had demonstrated little interest in the subject.

Our third objective is to note the principal findings embedded in this pioneering effort and the recommendations advanced to move toward accomplishing the congressional objectives of a comprehensive labor market information system. Finally, we will comment on the necessity of keeping user requirements, data collection, data analysis, and research capabilities in phase.

Although the Conservation of Human Resources Project at Columbia University had never been directly involved in the study of informational systems, it had, through its long years of manpower research, developed considerable knowledge about the strengths and weaknesses of manpower statistics for research and policy in both the public and private sectors. Moreover, during these years, it had increased its knowledge of the structure and functioning of labor markets, knowledge that was clearly relevant to the assignment at hand. Specifically, *The Peripheral Worker* by Dean Morse, *The Process of Work Establishment* by Marcia K. Freedman, *Education and Jobs: The Great Training Robbery* by Ivar E. Berg, *Changing Careers After Thirty-Five* by Dale L. Hiestand, and *Career Guidance* by Eli Ginzberg had directed attention to heretofore neglected dimensions of current labor market operations and fashioned new approaches to the study and analysis of these phenomena.

Our unhappiness with the quantity and particularly the quality of labor market information available for research, together with our deepening understanding of the complex forces operating in various labor markets, led us to agree to the request of the Manpower Administration of the U.S. Department of Labor that we undertake to develop a conceptual foundation for a labor market information system. This decision was made easier by the availability of Professor Boris Yavitz to head the project. He brought to this assignment considerable personal experience in the design and improvement of informational systems for large organizations in the private sector.

Professor Dean Morse served as Professor Yavitz's prinicpal associate and was responsible for the day-to-day operations of the project. He in turn was assisted by Mrs. Anna B. Dutka, who contributed significantly in the latter stages of the work when the manuscript was being revised for publication.

Chapters 5 through 8 are contributions by other members of the Conservation staff, who, drawing on their specialized knowledge and background, sought to illuminate by special probes selected issues involved in developing a strengthened labor market information system. These chapters include descriptions of the use by large employers of labor market information; the need for higher education to consider labor market information in making and revising its plans; the potentialities of strengthening career guidance through improved labor market information; and the priority needs of federal policy decision-makers for more relevant labor market information. The contributors were, respectively, Professors David Lewin, Ivar E. Berg, Eli Ginzberg, and James W. Kuhn.

These members of the Conservation staff, together with Professor Dale L. Hiestand and Drs. Marcia K. Freedman and Beatrice G. Reubens, served as a reference group for the authors as they went about their difficult task of drawing boundaries for their project and determining priority issues. While the authors are the architects as well as the builders of this study, the final output, representing the collaborative efforts of 10 staff members, reflects the work of the Conservation of Human Resources Project as a whole.

The final product is much more than a parochial Columbia effort. From start to finish Dr. Howard Rosen, Director of Manpower Research and Development of the Manpower Administration, and several members of his staff, particularly Joseph Epstein, Herman Travis, and Sheridan Maitland, worked closely with Yavitz and Morse. They proved helpful in many different ways, especially in illuminating the relations between the system in place with its diverse strengths and weaknesses and the ideal system, the delineation of which was the task of the researchers. Much of the credit for the relevance of the final product goes to these members of the Department of Labor staff.

The authors were also helped by inputs from two conferences. In November 1970, the Office of Manpower Research and Development called together all the contractors who were engaged on research projects funded under Section 106 of the Manpower Development and Training Act of 1968. As a result of the interchanges at this conference as well as through subsequent communications, the authors were helped to avoid pitfalls and to learn about promising areas for exploitation.

The second conference, which was larger and more extensive, took place at Tarrytown, New York, on June 2-4, 1971. The Conservation Project invited about 40 specialists knowledgeable in different manpower areas, including policy, research, and operations, to review a first draft of the present manuscript and to discuss the major themes to which it addressed itself. As a result of the incisive give-and-take at this conference, the authors recognized the need to revise their manuscript along the following lines: to pay more explicit attention to the encountered system; to improve their discussion of potential reforms by concrete references to labor market illustrations; to concentrate on the problems of strengthening the labor market information system in local areas where most individual, corporate, and governmental decision-making occurs; and finally to specify the sequential steps that should be taken to narrow the gap between the encountered system with its many weaknesses and a strengthened if not ideal system. Those who read the present work will be able easily to recognize the responsiveness of the authors to these conference recommendations.

This then is a sketch of the steps that led the Conservation of Human Resources Project to become involved in a study of the conceptual foundations of a labor market information system and that it followed in carrying out the assignment. The authors ran the risk of becoming mired in details, losing the forest for the trees, and thereby failing to be responsive to the charge of conceptualizing the foundations of a comprehensive system, while they had to avoid the opposite danger of becoming so immersed in delineating an ideal system that they might lose contact with the only system in existence, the encountered system that has to be improved if an ideal system is ever to be approximated.

The second question that this Foreword will explore is the concatenation of political, technological, and economic forces that led Congress to concern itself with such a seemingly peripheral subject as an improved labor market information system. The first and overriding fact is that Congress was concerned about the increasingly large sums it was appropriating for manpower programs in the absence of sharp delineation of the need for such programs and without a sound basis for judging the effectiveness with which the funds that it had appropriated were dispersed by the several levels of government and by nongovernmental agencies to bring worthwhile services to targeted groups. The total manpower appropriations in fiscal year 1968-69, when Section 106 was passed, exceeded $2 billion, about a tenfold increase in only six years. Moreover, Congress probably foresaw the likelihood of continuing increases in the years immediately following. These have in fact occurred; total appropriations for fiscal year 1971-72 amount to over $4 billion, and a further increment may bring this amount to $6 billion, subject to the passage of a welfare reform act.

Since Congress was unable to elicit hard facts from the several federal departments and agencies about the recipients of manpower services, it had little more than faith that its liberal funding for manpower programs was adding significantly to the employability and incomes of the participants. Moreover, faith was no answer to another primary problem to which many congressmen wanted an answer: how many people were there who, if funds were made available, might profit from one or another type of manpower service? Or what was the "universe of need" in relation to the scale of the present program? While the academic and governmental researchers, by torturing the existing data, were able to arrive at an estimate, they acknowledged and the congressmen understood that it was essential to improve the data base before introducing new legislation. A major spur to congressional interest in improved labor market information, therefore, was its desire to develop a firmer foundation for its own planning and programing and to exercise more effective control over the executive agencies that had responsibility for carrying out its dictates.

A second spur to congressional interest grew out of the computer revolution. The legislation referred to electronic data processing and telecommunications systems and placed repeated stress on job-matching programs. Here the interest and concern of Congress rested on the belief that, as a result of the electronics revolution, government would be able to provide better services both to the job seeker and to the employer in search of workers. The Federal-State Employment Service had long had the task of helping to bring together employers seeking workers and workers seeking jobs. But its success had been limited, because among other reasons its stock in trade had been the less attractive job vacancies and the less skilled members of the work force. Congress had supported the modernization of the Employment Service through the use of new technology and looked forward to improved clearance of the labor market as progress was made to develop job banks and improved worker-job matching systems. At a minimum, such improvements would help the hard-to-employ, who had become one of the principal client groups of the Employment Service. If the new technology could prove itself, Congress might expect that employers would make more use of the Employment Service. It should be noted parenthetically that in September 1971 President Richard M. Nixon directed all government contractors to list job vacancies with the Employment Service, thereby vastly increasing the number of higher-skilled and better-paying job openings to which the Employment Service could thereafter refer clients.

Congress also expected that the new technology would make a significant contribution to the improved planning involving occupational forecasting, employment trends, and economic and regional developments. The answers to these larger questions at national and subnational levels should be more readily forthcoming once use could be made of the rapidly improving computer technology.

Congress' growing awareness of the economic and human costs involved in unemployed and underemployed manpower resources was one more stimulus to its concern with a comprehensive labor market information system. The 1960s had demonstrated both the strength and the limitations of fiscal-monetary measures to bring the American economy to a high level of employment and to maintain tight labor markets. By 1968 it was increasingly clear to the members of Congress that even at the height of a boom, large numbers of Americans were unable to find and hold a job, and many more were unable to find jobs that would enable them to support their families adequately. Congress was concerned therefore with learning more about the barriers that prevent many people from achieving a maximum development of their employment potential, just as it wanted to learn more about the deficiencies and deficits on the demand side that contributed to current unemployment and underemployment. Congress expressed the belief and expectation that a strengthened labor market information system would help to highlight the changes in the institutional structures, which would aid in reducing the large-scale waste of human resources.

The positive response of Congress to a subject such as an improved labor market information system is now easier to understand. Congress wanted to play a more active role in appropriating and controlling expenditures for a program that had reached the multibillion-dollar level and that was headed higher. Congress believed that the new technology could provide improved manpower data for its own use as well as for all the other principals, including employers, workers, regional planners, and guidance personnel, in fact, all who had to make decisions, individual or collective, about the development and use of manpower resources. And it looked forward to important economic and human benefits from strengthened manpower policy and programing an improved labor market information system.

This brings us to the third question: What recommendations do the authors advance that are likely to lead to a strengthening of the labor market information system? It may be useful to start by mentioning what they do not recommend. For instance, they do not advocate scrapping the current system, although they analyze some of its shortcomings and call specific attention to many serious gaps. Next, they do not specify a rigid, definitive system, since they believe that any system must be subject to constant change if it is to meet effectively the demands of different users. They deny the validity of the concept of "comprehensiveness" and suggest the more modest term: a "multi-purpose" system.

In addition, they state that the improvement of the present system does not lie along the axis of a vast increase in new raw data collection, although they acknowledge that selective new data collection has a role to play in the improvement of the system.

Their first important recommendations, then, formulated here in nega-tives, are (1) not to scrap the existing system in the chimerical search for the ideal and (2) not to assume that the key to progress lies in the assembly of more and more data. Each of these paths can lead only to costly frustration and failure.

What then do they recommend? Their formulations are set out in detail in Chapter 10. We will limit ourselves here to a brief summary of their most important findings. First, they provide a framework within which the complex manpower employment system components and their interactions can be understood and its information needs analytically dealt with.

The primary thrust of the authors' recommendations is to encourage a demonstration effort to strengthen local labor market information collection and dissemination through a cooperative undertaking among the governmental and private and nonprofit sectors, with the last acting via a consortium of interested parties. They argue strongly that such a project could elicit the systematic input of valuable (and largely already available) information that would be made usable, under proper safeguards, to all cooperating members. This approach grows out of their conviction that government has come to the end of using its coercive powers to extract more information from the private sector for its own needs without giving the private sector much in return.

Specifically, the authors anticipate that this cooperative undertaking would help to eliminate the following defects in the existing local labor market informational system: the absence of a formal mechanism for locating, inven-torying, and categorizing the available data; the absence of a system for exchanging existing and new data among interested parties; the absence of a cost-benefit approach whereby producers of data would be encouraged to furnish more through the expectation of receiving more useful information in return; and the absence of a coordinating mechanism for such a clearing house effort.

The authors then design, at least in outline, how such a cooperative effort to improve the quality of local labor market information could be achieved, and they make the specific recommendation that the United States Employment Service (USES) serve as the coordinating agent.

In addition to this major thrust, the authors recommend that efforts be made to improve the quality of labor market information at the macro-level to underpin manpower policy and programing. Their primary stress in this regard is on improving the *quality* of the present data and minimizing the initial collection of more data; on identifying the principal categories of users and moving expeditiously from single-format, all-purpose to more specialized reports to meet their priority needs; and on moving as rapidly as possible to custom-made analyses in which important users, particularly the federal government, would be able to request one-time or periodic reports directly responsive to policy, programmatic, and control problems that are engaging its attention.

As the authors recognize, action along these three fronts would still leave the labor market information system far from being comprehensive, but it would represent a significant advance toward a more useful and responsive system. They correctly state that the only way to make progress is to identify the directions that will lead to the desired goal, to start moving in those directions, and to take periodic readings to ensure that the important labor market information that decision-makers need is being expanded and improved.

One of the major strengths of the Yavitz-Morse approach is its recognition of the necessity to keep the needs of users, the improvement of data, and the advances in conceptualization in tandem. They repeatedly stress the differences between data and information and between information and improved decisions and results. But they do not elaborate the critical role that improved conceptualization must play in the process of developing more effective information for improved decision-making. Since the Conservation Project's principal efforts have been directed to this end, it may be well to illustrate the critical role of improved conceptualization in the strengthening of labor market information. We will draw these illustrations from studies that the Conservation Project has recently completed or currently is preparing.

In their published and shortly to be published studies of metropolitan and suburban labor markets, Thomas Stanback and Richard Knight introduced new concepts and improvements on existing analytic devices, which enabled them to draw more from the existing data base. For instance, in *The Metropolitan Economy* (1970), Stanback and Knight developed a new category schema for cities and thus were able to demonstrate striking differences in the potential of cities for employment expansion. Moreover, by the single device of considering both employment increases and decreases, they were able to enhance our understanding of changes in different labor markets that would remain obscure as long as reliance was placed on netting-out differences. At the same time, their studies have called attention to the need for a revision of conventional categories of urban, rural nonfarm, and farm employment if we are to understand the dynamic transformations in labor markets.

The recent work of the Conservation Project on *Urban Unemployment* by Stanley Friedlander, *Aging in the Ghetto* by Dean Morse, *Work and Welfare* by Miriam Ostow, *Upgrading of Blue Collar and Service Workers* by Charles Brecher, all of which are scheduled for publication in the near future, calls attention to the need for a new accommodation between theory and information along the following axes: the necessity that labor market analysts broaden their analytical framework to take account of income flows from illicit and illegal work and from welfare; the extent to which large numbers of peripheral workers flow into and out of the labor market repeatedly during the course of the year; and the extent of different career mobility routes intrafirm, intraindustry, and intraarea, which are followed with or without accompanying changes in occupational status.

These few references to the interface between manpower research and manpower information were made to call attention to the need for improved conceptualization to advance progress in data collection, analysis, and dissemination. There is little point in adding vastly to our present data base unless advances are made in conceptualization. Moreover, the type of new and improved information that should be gathered and analyzed must be delineated in large measure by the needs of those who are working on the frontiers of manpower by improving our present conceptual framework and designing new approaches. Here is a strong reinforcement for the Yavitz-Morse recommendation that progress lies in the arena of improving the present labor market information system as quickly as possible so that it will be responsive to the special needs of different users, including the research community. If this effort of Yavitz and Morse speeds progress in this direction, all present and potential users of labor market information will be in their debt.

In Part I, a rationale and conceptual framework for governmental action designed to improve the flow of labor market information is presented. Chapter 1 discusses a number of recent transformations in the character of labor markets that in the authors' opinions have created a need for such action, from the point of view of the allocative efficiency of labor markets and from the point of view of the equity of labor market transactions.

Chapter 2 outlines a conceptual framework of a labor market information system that views actual job market transactions—hirings, dismissals, layoffs, and recalls—as the outcome of the interaction of two major subsystems, a manpower flow system and an employment flow system. A major point of interaction of these two subsystems is the job market proper, but there are other important linkages between them. By locating direct participants—i.e., employees and employers—and indirect participants or intermediaries—e.g., educational and training institutions, unions, public and private employment agencies—in a generalized spatial and temporal framework, strategic information flows become analytically distinguishable.

Chapter 3 is devoted to a discussion of some of the basic characteristics of information and information systems, in particular the distinction between information for planning and information for control, as they relate to questions of the detail, accuracy, and timeliness of data collection and the subsequent stages of data analysis and interpretation.

Against this background, five separate studies of important subsystems of the encountered labor market information system are presented in Part II. Chapter 4 focuses on job markets, concentrating on the informational implications of several different models of their operation. It emphasizes the importance of informal information networks and examines whether the provision of more job market information will lead to improved access to employment in favored sectors of the economy for individuals and groups who have encountered severe obstacles to such employment experience. In Chapter 5 the results of an investigation of the use of labor market information by a number of large urban employers is presented. According to informants in these firms, little direct use is made of labor market data generated by governmental agencies at the present time. The chapter presents suggestions for improved dissemination of labor market information to such users, along with suggestions that governmental agencies tap more efficiently information about the operation of local labor markets generated by such firms for their internal use. Chapter 6 examines the role of career guidance activities in the nation's educational institutions. The chapter focuses on linkages between career guidance activities and strategically important labor market intermediaries and participants in the labor market and points out that such linkages can be strengthened.

In the very recent past, increased attention has been paid to the role of institutions of higher education in preparing professional, technical, and other highly educated individuals for their subsequent careers. Chapter 7 centers on some of the major issues that have emerged and recommends that institutions of higher education learn to use labor market information in order to make critical decisions about programs and curricula. Continued neglect of the career needs of its graduates can only weaken the case that institutions of higher education are trying to make for greatly increased public support.

Chapter 8, an examination of the use of labor market information by federal policy-makers, concludes Part II. Based on interviews with individuals in such diverse agencies as the Council of Economic Advisers, the Office of Management and Budget, the Executive Office of the President, and various offices of the U.S. Department of Labor itself, the chapter points out a number of serious gaps in labor market information that adversely affect policy-making, both in the short run and in the longer run.

The first two parts of this volume examined, respectively, the elements of an information system's framework and the needs of several of its major user groups. In Part III we draw together a set of conclusions and recommendations for the development of an effective labor market information system.

We open, in Chapter 9, with a set of conclusions of the implications of a "comprehensive" labor market information system. We suggest "multipurpose" as perhaps a more realistic term than "comprehensive" and examine some of the reasons for such scaling down of terminology. Since any proposed or improved system must begin with what already exists, we review and summarize existing data sources and their formats. We also summarize the needs of the various users of the system. The chapter ends with a set of conclusions about a labor market information system and its users, which serves as the background for any further recommendations for action.

Our final Chapter 10 then proceeds to spell out these recommendations. We propose a dual-level attack, combining a "bottom-up" and "top-down" approach. We recommend simultaneous action on both the local and national levels of labor market information. This approach has been found effective and implementable in the design of many large-scale information systems.

At both levels we emphasize a phased and flexibly timed attack. Most attempts at designing complex systems in a single, glorious, all-at-once, "ideal" package have failed miserably. Our approach, instead, tries to identify the earmarks of an "idealized" (perhaps even unreachable) system but then proceeds to isolate a series of feasible, practical steps toward it.

The present study has been made possible through the support of the Manpower Administration of the U.S. Department of Labor. In addition to providing such support, individual members of the Department of Labor have provided generous assistance to us at a number of stages. In particular we would like to single out Joseph Epstein, Herman Travis, and Sheridan Maitland of the Office of Policy, Evaluation, and Research, with whom we have discussed on numerous occasions the general framework of our investigation and specific issues and problems. Without their contribution to the spirit and the day-to-day implementation of the study, the principal authors and their colleagues would have been sorely tried in delimiting the scope of their efforts. We should also at the outset recognize their encouragement to us to hold fast to the intention that our work be conceptual in character and to make the conceptual framework as broad as possible.

In addition to these three men, we have had the assistance of other individuals from other parts of the Department of Labor, too numerous to mention by name. The generosity of those who took time to discuss problems with us and to read drafts of the study puts us very much in their debt. We have also been the beneficiaries of several conferences, in particular a conference held in Tarrytown, New York, in June 1971, to discuss an earlier version of this report. At this conference experts drawn from industry, government, and the academic community, discussed the general question of labor market information from many points of view, and our final report bears many, if unacknowledged in detail, evidences of the stimulating and imaginative contributions made by conference participants.

Finally we owe much to our colleagues at the Conservation of Human Resources Project of Columbia University, several of whom contributed chapters: Professors James Kuhn, Ivar Berg, David Lewin, and Eli Ginzberg. The entire staff discussed our ongoing work on numerous occasions. Professor Dale Hiestand and Dr. Marcia Freedman were participants at the conference in Tarrytown. Dr. Beatrice Reubens provided detailed criticism of the draft report. In addition to such formal assistance, the principal investigators were able to call upon individual members of the Conservation of Human Resources Project staff for countless informal discussions, and we are deeply grateful to them for their willingness to suffer our interruption of their own work.

We should add that our general approach to the subject reflects the work of the Conservation Project over many years. It is quite frankly based on a conception of the operation of labor markets that emphasizes the important role of public policy in mitigating the inequities and inefficiencies, the insidious and often calamitous effects of discriminatory barriers and of imperfect linkages between public and private institutions. It concentrates on those groups and individuals who find it most difficult to gain access to the benefits of stable employment at good wages in jobs with well-defined progression upward in skill and remuneration.

Although this conception of labor markets and public policy is reflected in the work of individual members of the Conservation Project, it is preeminently the contribution of the Project's Director, Dr. Eli Ginzberg. Only the principal authors of the following report can know how much they relied on his judgement and imagination. To the extent that we have succeeded in relating the issue of a comprehensive labor market information system to the fundamental character of the nation's labor markets and to the intermediary institutions that are part of the immensely complicated process by which the nation's demand for labor is matched to its supply over time, to the extent that we have been able to keep clearly in mind the relation between the operation of these labor markets and the effects, both actual and potential, of public policy and practice, we have reflected his guidance.

# LIST OF FIGURES

Figure

# ELEMENTS OF
# A CONCEPTUAL
# FRAMEWORK

# 1

# INTRODUCTION
# AND STATEMENT
# OF THE CASE

The Congress of the United States, amending the Manpower Development and Training Act of 1968, asked the Secretary of Labor to take steps to create a comprehensive labor market information system. As described in the enabling legislation, the "comprehensive labor market information system" envisaged by Congress will include the following kinds of information: First, information, on a *national, state,* local, or other "appropriate basis," is to be provided on

(1) the nature and extent of impediments to the maximum development of individual exployment potential including the number and characteristics of all persons requiring manpower services;

(2) job opportunities and skill requirements;

(3) labor supply in various skills;

(4) occupational outlook and employment trends in various occupations; and

(5) in cooperation and after consultation with the Secretary of Commerce, economic and business development and location trends.

This information is to be provided "in a timely fashion" to meet the needs of *"public* and *private* users" in "recruitment, counseling, education, training, placement, job development and other appropriate activities" (emphasis added).

Secondly, the system will provide information on *"available job opportunities* throughout the United States on a National, State, local or other appropriate basis for use in *public* and *private* job placement, education and training, and related activities and in connection with job matching programs" (emphasis added).

3

These job-matching programs are to be the third major elements in the system. In them, "the qualifications of *unemployed, underemployed, and low-income* persons" are to be matched with "employer requirements and job opportunities," again on a "National, State, local or other appropriate basis." In the job-matching program, "maximum use" will be made of "electronic data processing and telecommunication systems" (emphasis added)[1].

While engaging in a major effort, now well under way, to create a system of job banks and computerized job-matching systems as an integral part of a labor market information system, the Department of Labor also has supported several research projects designed to cast light on a number of issues involved in the creation of a comprehensive labor market information system.

In addition to quite specific problems, for example those arising in the development of computerized job-matching facilities or those that emerge in designing a local labor market information system, individuals entrusted with the task of developing a comprehensive labor market information system for the nation as a whole confront a number of knotty conceptual problems. The present investigation is an effort to come to grips with some of them.

* * * *

An issue, preliminary to any attempt to sketch the boundaries and characteristics of a comprehensive labor market information system, is whether it is indeed at all appropriate for government to be engaged in such a task. Is the congressional mandate to the Secretary of Labor justified? Most of Chapter 1 is devoted to this question. If an affirmative answer could not have been given, the remaining chapters of this report would have been merely an exercise in how to do something that in fact should not be done. Needless to say, our answer is strongly affirmative.

Some related questions are also best discussed in this chapter. Does a labor market information system rest on a particular set of values, certain preconceptions about human behavior, and the role of government, many of which tend to be implicit?

If so, what are the implications of these values and preconceptions? What kinds of effects do they have on the design and implementation of an information system? Do they tend to introduce biases into the system? If so, what kind of biases are created and how may they be counteracted?

What purposes, ultimately, is the comprehensive labor market information system, mandated by Congress, to fulfill? Who are to receive the potential benefits? Who are to pay the inevitable costs?

Such issues are bound to arise; and the more comprehensive and effective the labor market information system, the more costly its operation; the more pervasive its effects on labor markets and the fortunes of individuals and groups within the society, the sooner they must be faced and answers provided. Chapter 1 does not pretend to provide such answers. In the nature of the case, it is no more than a preliminary survey of such issues.

4

# RECENT SOCIAL AND ECONOMIC CHANGES AND
# THEIR LABOR MARKET INFORMATION IMPLICATIONS

Only in recent years has the issue of comprehensive labor market information been raised. An economy based on private property and individual choice, with a minimum of intervention on the part of government, theoretically generates a body of information, in the form of prices of inputs and outputs, that provides individuals with the basis for rational action.

At this point the authors feel that in the interest of clarity a semantic distinction should be drawn. Many students of the labor market have been accustomed to referring to the arena in which employers and job seekers conclude their transactions as the "labor market." On the other hand, the same students, when they have a much broader frame of reference in mind, may still use the same term. We shall use the term "job market" when we mean the specific arenas in which job transactions take place, and we shall reserve the expression "labor market" to refer to the entire set of interlinked institutions and processes that determine the flows of job opportunities and manpower in both the short and the long run. These distinctions are developed at greater length in Chapter 2.

With this distinction made between "labor market" and "job market," it may be useful to ask whether any transformations either in the general nature of the economy itself or specifically in the performance of labor markets themselves, or, alternatively, in our conception of the proper functioning of the economy, have taken place in recent decades that would justify provision of both "labor market" information and "job market" information by government. In the following pages we will indicate in summary fashion several transformations that in our opinion do make it reasonable to ask government to devote increasing attention to the construction of a comprehensive labor market information system.

Since World War II the rate of change of technology, of tastes, of location of jobs and residence, of educational attainment, to name some of the more prominent elements, has been pronounced. Many people have had to make frequent and drastic changes in their behavior, and the signals given by price changes, and in particular by wage changes, are often no longer prompt enough or adequate for the task.

Just as the consumer lacks an informational base that permits him to cope efficiently with the rapidly increasing technical complexity of products, the proliferation of models, and the sophistication (and deception) of marketing practices, making it very difficult for him to allocate his income rationally, so it can be asserted that there is also an inadequate informational base for the allocation of productive resources that now take place in a technological and institutional environment much more complex than that of the nineteenth century. Moreover, just as many consumption decisions involve long-term horizons, so do decisions about productive activity.

It seems likely that an increasing awareness of economic and social interdependence may make us much less willing to tolerate the misallocation of labor that can lead certain groups into dead-end occupations.* The plight of blacks who have migrated from the rural South to the cores of a number of the country's largest cities during the past few decades has been well documented. Policies and related programs will need to be built on increasingly detailed and comprehensive information about the economic and social conditions of the urban cores and about their labor markets.

Another transformation of the economy and society that has heightened our awareness of labor market informational requirements is the ever-increasing replacement of the extended family by the nuclear family. A very important part of labor market information has been traditionally transmitted by means of a network of family relationships. With dispersion of families, this kind of information is less relevant, and this is particularly the case for both ends of the scale: the most mobile parts of our population, which tend to be the most highly educated and skilled as well as the most disadvantaged, least skilled, and least informed (in the latter case, families are often torn by migration and desertion and those family members who remain are often poor sources of information).

It is now necessary to develop channels of labor market information to make up for what once was efficiently transmitted between family members. It is not a coincidence that some of the most sophisticated channels for communication of such information have been developed by professional societies. Further, the tendency of corporations to develop universalistic and impersonal hiring practices, particularly for managerial ranks, is pronounced, and the labor market for such personnel is more and more a national market.

The increased suburbanization of our society with its dispersal of population and economic activity has undermined another prime source of labor market information—friends. In a situation where it is not uncommon for neighbors to be literally strangers, suburbs cannot generate much labor market information for their residents who must rely increasingly, as we have seen, on informational networks created by their professional contacts and societies.

On the other hand, we are now beginning to find that much of the area surrounding our largest cities are becoming dominated by what can be termed "working class suburbs." The informational implications of such developments are fairly clear and potentially dangerous. So long as the corporations whose work force lives in such suburbs prosper, there is little need for labor market information in these areas. If, on the other hand, the corporations find themselves cutting down their labor force, the individuals who live in such suburbs often find themselves isolated from labor market information on the one hand and tied by homeownership to a fixed location on the other. Such individuals in too many instances do not have a highly developed professional informational network connected to national labor market conditions to fall back on, and it may no longer be possible for them to cope unaided with the informational requirements of the new labor markets.

Affluence has another effect, however, one that is likely to become more significant with the passage of time. It gives many individuals greater freedom

_____

*That is, prices may do a reasonable job for short-term employment decisions but fail miserably in the long-run.

and more options and diminishes the pressure felt by some young people to make an early commitment to career or any commitment at all. Indeed, this raises the possibility that chief among the transformations that have recently taken place that have profound labor market informational implications is a change in values that has altered the way important segments of the population perceive the labor market and therefore has produced significant changes in the kinds of information that can gain access to these groups.

At a recent conference the discussion at one point turned to the difficulties that have been encountered in disseminating labor market information to black youth. One of the discussants, Paul Bullock of the University of California, declared that

> not only is the nature of the information and even the style in which the information is presented important, but also the question of who presents the information—the image of this person or this institution.[2]

To the extent that major subgroups of the population have differing value images, particularly of the labor market itself, there are apt to be marked differences in the way the various groups *receive* and *perceive* what in fact are objectively the same messages about labor markets. What gets past the various filters and what distortions take place are questions about which labor market information specialists are beginning to accumulate experience, largely from observing how different are the reactions of various groups to what is ostensibly the same bit of information.

To return to other possible transformations in the nature of the economy or of labor markets that have major informational implications, it may be the case that there has been a steady decrease in the number and significance of labor markets that can be reasonably viewed as competitive. If so, this circumstance would have major informational implications. In highly competitive markets, individuals and firms do not have to engage in any very extensive investigation to determine the demand or supply curve of whatever it is they are selling or buying but can instead take prices as given. But, where there are monopolistic elements in the market situation, a great deal more information is desirable but often very difficult to obtain.

Another transformation in labor markets with important informational implications is the changing composition of the labor force itself during the last few decades, which is likely to continue in the decades to come. Chief among these changes is the rapid increase in the portion of the labor force that is made up of women and, among these women, the rapid increase in the portion who are married and who have reentered the labor force.

The decrease in the labor force participation rates of black women, particularly noticeable in the case of the younger age groups, is obviously connected with the increased unwillingness of black women to accept menial and dead-end employment experience. This development means that training programs and related labor market informational programs directed at them will have to be built on a recognition of their changed attitude toward themselves and their relation to the world of work.

Basic institutional and conceptual changes, for example changes in the nature of the welfare system or in the income restrictions placed on Social Security recipients, will necessarily bring about new informational problems as these institutional changes alter the ways in which people perceive their relation to the world of work. Changes in the nature of the corporation and labor organizations, changes in laws and customs, and finally changes in the nature of our conception of information itself and in information technology are bound to be of profound significance in determining the appropriate boundaries for what is included in the term "labor market information."

Quite aside from other transformations that might justify an attempt to create a more comprehensive and systematic body of labor market information than we now possess is the transformation in our conception of what constitutes the proper role of government with respect to the economy, in other words, our conception of economic policy.

Several years ago the late E. Wight Bakke argued that a national economic policy necessarily implied what he called a "positive labor market policy."[3] Bakke pointed out that the execution of such a labor market policy demands a wide range of general and specific information about labor markets. He emphasized that such a labor market policy must be integrated with general economic policy and that it must be particularly active on the demand side, since it is only through the creation of demand for jobs that actual employment is brought about.

It is not enough, according to Bakke, to create a supply of labor. An active labor market policy must be based on informed judgments about future demand for labor, relating labor market developments to developments in other parts of the economy. Moreover, labor market policy should rank equally with monetary, fiscal, and trade policy.

## THE RATIONALE OF GOVERNMENT-SUPPLIED LABOR MARKET INFORMATION

Labor market information can be divided into numerous categories. The kinds of labor market information that bear directly on the decisions of employers and employees, actual and potential, often differ from the kinds of information needed for decisions made by people other than the direct participants in actual job markets. The distinction between these two kinds of information is basic to much of what is contained in succeeding chapters and will be developed in some detail in Chapters 2 and 3. It is sufficient for our present purposes to note the distinction in broad outline.

The provision by government action of these two types of information is in several fundamental respects based on quite different considerations. Let us take up first the case of information bearing directly on labor market transactions between employer and job seeker. In what sense are such labor market transactions any different from other economic transactions? If the government is not called on to provide information for these other economic transactions, is there something about the nature and the functioning of the job market that justifies the government acting to provide information directly to the job seeker and the employer?

Several affirmative answers can be given. The first of these centers on the similiarity of labor market information possessed by the individual job seeker to what has come to be called intellectual capital in general. These include the skills and aptitudes that increase his productivity, accumulated by his incurring the costs of education and training. In this sense the direct money costs and the indirect opportunity costs of job search on the part of the job seeker lead to an increase in the productivity of a worker, just as education and training do, because they enable a worker to come closer to matching his skills and aptitudes to that employment that will offer him the highest return.

Economists have come to realize that, as with other forms of capital, neither the distribution of intellectual capital in the form of labor market information nor its total amount is necessarily optimal. Imperfections in the labor and capital markets can prevent individuals, certain demographic and geographical groups, and perhaps the entire labor force from acquiring the proper amount of labor market information.

It would be very difficult, although obviously desirable, to estimate the private and the social gains that would accrue to individuals, or to society as a whole, if job market information inadequacies could be eliminated. Among the many problems involved in such estimates are the proper time horizon for the estimates and the proper rate of discount to apply to government investments in information. For example, if an individual makes a decision as a young man to accept employment at a job that provides him with less income than he might have otherwise secured but at the same time provides him with more on-the-job training than he might have obtained elsewhere, it is difficult to determine the cumulative effect of his decision on lifetime earnings and job satisfaction.

Another problem that must be faced in trying to estimate the value of additional job market information is whether the provision of such information merely shifts jobs from one group of individuals to another, so that one individual's gain is another's loss, with no net social gain, or whether, by permitting individuals collectively to match more closely their innate and acquired abilities, aptitudes, and personalities to the requirements of the employers, the total productivity of the entire group is raised. It is also possible that, in inflationary situations resulting largely from rising labor costs, the provision of more job market information would not only hold down such costs and increase worker productivity but also increase the level of employment as well, but, again, the evaluation of such gains would be enormously difficult.

In terms of an individual's own career path and the associated income streams, another issue needs to be faced.

At the point in their development when investments in human capital must usually be made, individuals may lack information about lifetime income profiles of occupations for which they have aptitudes and they may be still so uncertain about their vocational interests that decisions to spend what may amount to four or more years and many thousands of dollars in an educational and training program cannot be made properly.

Moreover, temporary economic conditions may postpone forever investments in human capital just as fortunate combinations of circumstances may make possible investments that otherwise would never have taken place. A portion of an entire generation of Americans was denied adequate opportunities for investment in human capital by the Great Depression of the 1930s, just as a succeeding generation, or at least those fortunate enough to survive World War II intact, were enabled by the GI Bill of Rights to invest more than they otherwise probably would have had in various forms of education and training.

Finally, and perhaps most fundamental, investments by individuals in human capital depend to a large extent on their access to the capital market and on family information about the advantages of different occupations. It is obvious that lack of capital within a family with which to finance investments in education is apt to be combined with both lack of information about the value of such investments and formidable social and cultural barriers that make it difficult for a young person to decide to forgo immediate income in favor of such investments. But along with differences among families in ability and inclination to supply youth with such capital is a marked difference in the ease of access of individuals to capital supplied by institutions outside the family. Students, teachers, guidance personnel, and school administrators all may be influenced by faulty conceptions about operation of labor markets and inadequate or wrong information about careers, occupations, and access to financial assistance for post-high school education.

But, even if a young person is correctly informed and guided, he may find that the capital market does not serve him adequately even when it makes tuition loans available to him, if it does not at the same time provide income supplements. Here the problem may be not the student's lack of information about loan programs but rather the lack of information on the part of program formulators about the target population; whatever the cause, the result is again a misallocation of human capital.

Just as investments in human capital in the form of education are in some cases misallocated or less than optimal, so may investments in labor market information be less than optimal. An individual's exploration of the job market can be viewed as a set of probes designed to raise his productivity by improving the match between his personal qualities and job opportunities. In technical terms, he should search for information until the discounted value of the additional income stream associated with the additional search effort is no longer greater than the accumulated cost of the search effort.

Faulty information, however, may distort the process of search so that an individual in fact either does not search long enough or searches too long. In particular, an individual is unlikely to be able to see clearly how a particular decision to accept a job is related to lifetime income. The vaguer the future is, the more it becomes discounted and, other things being equal, the shorter the job search.

But individuals also spend too little or too much effort on job search because the length of time they can afford to devote to the accumulation of job market information is affected by their access to the capital market. One effect of unemployment insurance, for example, has been to enable an individual to prolong his job search. Since people have unequal amounts of liquid assets and unequal access to public and private resources with which to finance job search, it is inevitable that there are marked differences in the amount of job search that people, otherwise similar, are willing and able to make.

The point of these remarks is that an unequal distribution of assets available to finance job searching will result in an unequal distribution of labor market information derived from job searching. There is every reason therefore to conclude that the distribution and amount of such labor market information in the hands of individuals is not optimal.

Rather than search actively from one employer to another for employment, in the process accumulating information about the job market, an individual can turn the task of accumulating job market information over to another individual, purchasing from individuals who specialize in the accumulation of such information what he would otherwise have to accumulate through his own efforts. In effect that is what a private employment agency does for job seeker and employer. Access to labor market information in the hands of private employment agencies, however, is limited to those who can afford to pay for these services or whose employer-to-be will pay. This constraint is reinforced by the fact that such agencies usually limit their services to clients with specified educational and other characteristics, among which such attributes as race, national origin, social status, and similar discriminatory features often loom large.

To sum up, a strong case can be made for government action to provide individuals with job market information. However, the particular types of compensatory programs that would operate most efficiently and equitably are not so immediately obvious. Should the major effort of such programs be to improve the efficiency of the allocation of labor in the short-run, or should the programs aim more at long-run and cumulative effects? Should programs sacrifice some amount of short- or long-run efficiency in allocation of labor in the interest of equity by, for example, deliberately aiming to provide information primarily to those who have suffered from a relative lack of labor market information?

Even more fundamental questions can be raised. Can programs designed to compensate for past labor market information deprivation alter to a significant extent the actual pattern of allocation of labor? How important, in other words, would improved access to labor market information be for those individuals and groups whose employment experience has been erratic and confined to relatively poor jobs? Do programs that provide additional labor market information to such individuals need to be supplemented by other types of intervention in the labor market designed to improve its equity?

The focus of the discussion up to this point has been on the provision of additional labor market information by the government to individuals to improve their access to desirable jobs. This type of information, general or specific as the case may be, is utilized in the making of micro-decisions. Information of this type can be directed either to job seekers or to employers.

In general, however, it seems clear that it will in many cases be necessary for such information programs to be tied closely to other types of labor market intervention—training programs, antidiscrimination legislation, relocation subsidies, and perhaps compulsory job listing.

There is another argument of quite a different character that supports the provision of labor market information by government. It asserts that some kinds of labor market information are public goods, similar in economic essentials to fire and police protection or perhaps, more directly, to the provision of public education. The collection and dissemination of information about national unemployment rates illustrates this aspect of labor market information. Although an individual employer or employee might find such information useful, he cannot possibly afford to collect the data that would enable him to determine the national rate, and it is likely that, even if he could, it would be difficult for him to keep this information to himself. In other words, the collection of such information requires the resources of government, and, once collected, the value of this information can best be reaped by the widest possible dissemination.

Government agencies, national, state, and local as the case may be, intervene in numerous ways in the operation of the labor market through activities that range from the traditional placement operations of USES to the extensive training and job development efforts that have developed under the impetus of the Manpower Development and Training Act of 1968 and other employment and antipoverty measures of the 1960s.

Beyond such direct intervention in the operation of local and national labor markets through placement and training operations, federal, state, and local governments engage in a number of activities and make decisions that have profound impact on labor markets both nationally and locally. Thus, at one extreme of governmental activity are the decisions of local governmental bodies to attract new industries or determine the location of industry and residential locational patterns through such means as zoning and tax policy. At the other are those governmental decisions that have the entire economy as their frame of reference. Primarily *macro-decisions*, they involve the use of fiscal and monetary policies and are designed to influence the level of GNP and the rate of growth of the economy. They are in large part predicated upon their anticipated effects on labor markets and particularly, in a time of inflationary pressures, upon their effects on the general wage level. Included in these macro-decisions are those decisions of government that indirectly, if not purposefully, have powerful repercussions on local, regional, or national labor market conditions, for example, a national highway program or housing program.

## PROVIDING MACRO-LABOR MARKET INFORMATION

A form of intervention by government in labor markets, then, is the provision of large amounts of labor market information, much of it macro in character.

There has been a long tradition of collection by government agencies of data that bear on the operation of labor markets. The Bureau of Labor Statistics (BLS) is the focus of much of this fact-finding activity, but the BLS does not monopolize the field.* The departments of labor of the individual states have for many decades collected information about the labor markets that come under their jurisdiction. Moreover, much of what the BLS does collect has obvious significance far beyond the boundaries of labor markets themselves. Price indexes are merely one, if a particularly important, example of information, collected by a governmental agency primarily concerned with the collection and dissemination of labor market information, that has profound effects on decisions of public and private agencies and individuals concerned with matters outside the labor market as conventionally viewed.

The range and variety of labor market information collected by various government agencies, federal, state, and local, is impressive and represents a very significant proportion of the total statistical efforts of government in the United States. The costs of these programs runs into several hundreds of millions of dollars each year, and the prospect is that their costs will increase, perhaps markedly, in the decades to come. Not only is the money cost of the program sizable, but the cost in time to respondents—business units, government agencies, and private individuals—can in some instances be truly burdensome.

It is only natural, therefore, that questions should be raised about the value of these information-gathering efforts. Some of these are

(1) Who benefits from the various information-gathering programs? How do benefits relate to costs?

(2) If a particular program is justified, should it be extended and by how much?

(3) Conversely, if a program on its present scale is not worthwhile, would a smaller (or larger) effort in the same direction prove justified?

(4) What new programs should be undertaken? How rapidly should they be introduced?

(5) If a program is not currently justified in terms of its use, is this because the data being collected are inherently not worth collecting, or is it because insufficient resources are devoted to the analysis of the data or insufficient resources are directed at the dissemination of the product or because related labor market information is not available?

The above list is inevitably incomplete, but it does serve to emphasize that many of the questions that might be asked about specific labor market information-gathering programs often represent implicit questions about whether the total information-gathering effort is sufficiently integrated and comprehensive in character.

A major problem of labor market information related to governmental decision-making and program implementation arises from the fact that govern-

---

*Nor does the BLS usually collect information directly. Rather, it depends on other agencies, for example, the Bureau of the Census, to carry out the surveys on which its reports and analyses are based.

ment decisions and programs take place on many levels and are made by a number of governmental agencies. The problem of coordination of programs and information generated by these programs, particularly when they have many-faceted goals, is one of the chief arguments for a constant effort to make labor market information systems more comprehensive and more coordinated and for answering the questions raised above from a systems point of view.

We wish to emphasize that we are not arguing that government should provide all labor market information. Rather, we believe that government can play a strategically important role, particularly in locating and bridging those gaps in labor market information systems that cannot be filled by private initiative and in assisting those agencies and firms, already devoting important resources to the development of labor market information, to link information-gathering and disseminating activities together in such a fashion as to reap the maximum possible external benefits. The actual organizational forms that might be utilized for these purposes could be widely varied, ranging from the purely public agency to the governmentally subsidized but privately operated organizations, to the wholly privately supported, but cooperative, activities of industries, trade unions, trade associations, and professional organizations. Bank clearing houses stand out as a most successful prototype of such a cooperative organization.

## A VALUE-FREE LABOR MARKET INFORMATION SYSTEM?

Finally, we believe it important to raise the following explicit question: Is a labor market information system a neutral affair, simply a tool to be used by decision-makers to enable them to improve the results of their decisions? In our opinion, deeply embedded in the fundamental concepts of a labor market information system are certain basic values of our society. Moreover, the labor market information specialist works within the limits of these values, even though at times he may not be aware of them. These values determine what data, out of an enormously large set of data, he believes to be worth collecting and analyzing.

Thus a liberal democratic society whose economy is in principle organized on the basis of free markets will value efficiency, equality of opportunity, social mobility, and freedom of choice. Armed with information the common man is supposed to be able to make most of the decisions that are necessary for his well-being. Such a society tends to believe that most of the ills of the society are the product of ignorance and that a little information is better than none at all.

It is easy to transfer these general attitudes toward information to the specific arena of the labor market. If our labor markets are not working efficiently, if they have inequitable elements, let the flow of information improve and the operation of the labor markets will become at once more efficient and more equitable. If unemployment rates are too high, this is in part because barriers to the flow of information about job vacancies prevent job seekers from finding out about them. If young people flounder in the labor market when they first enter it, prepare them by giving them information about occupations.

The system will work reasonably well if people are informed, mobile, and rational. It will be efficient, and the sources of inequity in the system will be more or less clear cut. Either people start the race with unequal inherited endowments or through bad luck or mismanagement of their endowments they fall behind.

Difficulties, theoretical and practical, arise when people and things are not mobile. And, since information, like everything else, is in fact not always accurate and available and never really a free good, people cannot always be well informed. Incurring costs of one kind or another in order to acquire information, they will on occasion be unemployed even though more information, too costly from their point of view, would have told them of the existence of a job further down the road.

That the efficiency of a free market system depends to a significant degree on an adequate flow of information has long been recognized by economists. The recent work of Kenneth Arrow emphasizes the importance of information and reminds us that uncertainty and lack of information are much the same state of affairs. Thus, for example, because it is difficult for automobile manufacturers to transmit sufficient information about the quality of their products to consumers, consumers are only imperfectly informed and it becomes impossible for the manufacturer whose product is in fact superior to capitalize fully on his edge in quality. The net effect of information imperfection in the automobile market is therefore to lower the quality of the product.

What Arrow in effect is saying is that, while consumers may be quite well informed about certain characteristics of automobiles such as price, horsepower, weight, and so forth, they lack information about important quality dimensions that, if available, would lead them to alter their patterns of consumption. Arrow's suggestions about the operation of the automobile market can be readily translated into labor market terms.

In recent years there have been persistent complaints about the quality of jobs as well as the quality of cars.[4] If in fact it is difficult to transmit information about job quality (while at the same time easy to transmit information about such things as wage rates), then it may be the case that those employers who offer superior working conditions may not be able to capitalize on such offers by attracting workers whose superior productivity would justify the increased expense associated with these superior working conditions, just as the automobile manufacturer who offers a superior vehicle cannot capitalize adequately on this superiority because consumers are not adequately informed about it.

In other words, the effects of imperfections in labor market information may be just as pervasive (although not widely understood) as imperfections in the flow of information in commodity markets. In the case of automobile markets, we have witnessed a rash of private and public efforts to contend with what are alleged to be serious product defects. Naderism is but one aspect of this new concern. Another is an increased willingness on the part of society to call on government to be both watchdog and information dispenser. Perhaps we may anticipate analogous governmental activities in the labor market if the level of concern about quality of jobs continues to rise.

## COSTS AND BENEFITS: INDIVIDUAL AND SOCIAL

A society changeless in technique and tastes would not need a highly developed information system. Indeed one of the prime functions of an information system is to tell people that things tomorrow will differ from what they are today. All change involves costs, as well as benefits, and the working assumption of an economy organized around individual choice is that the individual will bear the costs of change unless it is clearly perceived that these costs are intolerable or inequitably distributed.

In the past it has on occasion been difficult for us to accept the fact that some types of costs are "social" rather than individual in character and hence ought to be borne by society in general. And, similarly, we have often been unwilling to shift choices from the individual to larger groups unless there seems to be an overwhelming case for such a shift. This predisposition may also cause us to fail to provide the necessary flow of information to those entrusted with making decisions for larger social groups—the city, the county, the state, or the country as a whole. The information system may be so constructed, in line with this fundamental belief in the importance of individual choice (and its corollary, individual responsibility for the cost of failure and benefits of success), that in the first instance it may not communicate costs to higher levels of decision-making adequately and in the second may not register properly the social gains that might arise from a shift of the locus of choice from the individual to a larger social group.*

## THE VALUE OF INFORMATION

There is another value embedded in our information system, innocent in appearance but potentially pernicious. We have already alluded to it in our reference to the common belief that some information is better than none. It is significant that another part of folk wisdom maintains that a little knowledge is a dangerous thing. The problem of a little information is essentially the problem of bias. Its effects can easily be illustrated. Let us assume that the true state of affairs is that a number of occupations, ranging from high skilled to low skilled, are open to a group of black teen-agers of a given education level. If a formal labor market information system designed to improve their labor market decisions has information only about the openings in low-skilled occupations, it will bias their decisions in the direction of these occupations. In this case we would get a poorer kind of decision on the average then if this same group were given no information at all but rather, by sampling the labor

---

*If there is any single kind of information that is most generally lacking, it is in all probability information dealing with "social" costs and benefits. Admittedly these are very difficult to measure. But until recent years we seem to have been scarcely aware of their existence, even though economists like Alfred Marshall made them a central part of their economic analysis. Our national income accounts still simply ignore the existence of social costs and benefits.

market, tried to discover for themselves the probabilities of being hired at various skill levels.

The case of the black teen-agers in our example might be even more unfortunate if, in addition to the information about access to low-skilled occupations that our putative formal information system provides them, black teen-agers have access to another information system, let us say the informal labor market information system that has grown up in the black community, based largely on past experiences of blacks with discriminatory barriers that prevent their access to high-skilled occupations. In this case one information system, the informal, has already told them not to bother to apply to employers offering employment in high-skilled occupations, and we now add to this underlying information an additional input that tells the teen-ager that he can get employment if he is willing to accept low-skilled occupations. We have, almost certainly, led him to apply for jobs at only one skill level. If the true state of affairs is that discriminatory barriers are being lowered across the board, we have made it almost certain that he will not engage in the kind of exploratory behavior in the labor market that would, over a period of time, lead to some alteration in his perceptions of the way the labor market operates. By accepting the idea that an increment of information is a good thing, no matter how selective it may be or unrepresentative of the true state of affairs, we have unwittingly brought about the opposite of our intention to increase the employment prospects of black teen-agers!

We can draw several general conclusions from this example. The first is that it is essential that the designers of an informational system that is going to be superimposed on an existing system—in this case a formal labor market information system is going to be added to an informal labor market information system—understand thoroughly the content and form of the underlying informal information system and take them into account in setting up the formal system. If not, the effects of gaps in the one system may simply be reinforced by gaps in the other and may confirm the misinformation that initially produced bad decisions.

Another consideration should be kept in mind. All information is ultimately derived from past events. Formal information systems can "force" an updating at given times and can also be the basis of complex forecasting models. By contrast, informal systems are very immune to updating, and their most commonly used model for forecasting is very simple, the assumption of *continuity:* Tomorrow will be the same as yesterday.

The second conclusion is somewhat less apparent. It has to do with the nature of informal information systems in general, but it probably has a particularly strong application to labor market information systems. An informal information system is apt to be made up of inputs of information that have been accumulated over a long period of time. Its embodiment in any one individual represents the slow accretion of bits and pieces of knowledge, some parts very closely integrated, others more loosely tied to the main structure. Much of this information is only partly conscious, at best.

From our point of view it is essential to keep in mind that parts of the information system are firmly rooted in the past. It helps to explain the fact

17

that behavior always tends to seem to be conservative; it is part of what we mean when we say that custom produces a considerable amount of inertia in any system of social interaction. A formal information system must reflect to some, probably large, extent our informal information system, if for no other reason than that these informal systems have already been responsible for a good part of our awareness of what we believe the real situation to be. Instead of bringing to light the important *changes* in the structure of reality, the formal system may, if it is not carefully designed, simply reinforce the old vision of the social order, and the information inputs that it adds may be primarily of a tactical rather than a strategic character. In this sense, then, it may in fact act as a profoundly conservative instrument, and, in situations where the social structure is in fact rapidly and radically changing, the formal information system may provide the decision-maker, on whatever level he may be, with very little truly appropriate information about how to cope with the changing structure of reality.

## SUMMARY

The burden of most of Chapter 1 is that a strong case can be made for energetic action by the federal government to provide labor market information on a number of different levels—to individual workers and employers; governmental agencies and policy-makers, local, regional, and federal; and a host of labor market intermediaries. A number of recent transformations in our economic and social life reinforce long-standing beliefs of economists that labor market information has important externalities that justify its collection and dissemination by government.

But, since the creation of a comprehensive labor market information system would have such powerful and widespread effects on national economic policy, on the plans and policies of state and local governments, on the decisions of employers, and on the life chances of employees, it behooves those individuals and agencies on whom falls the task of designing and implementing a comprehensive labor market information system to be as clear as possible about the preconceptions and values that enter into the system they create. It would be an ironic waste of effort if we were to impose on a labor market information system social and economic tasks that it cannot possibly fulfill and as a consequence fail to take those measures that are in fact appropriate.

# 2

# THE SYSTEMS
# APPROACH

When viewed against an inclusive conception of the flows of manpower and job opportunities, the conventional economic model of an employer/employee exchange appears far too narrow, static, and oversimplified. Thinking in terms of such a confined model not only is limiting but also can actually prove misleading. It focuses attention on only one element or phase of a complex and dynamic process.

A far more useful view is provided by visualizing a transaction in the job market as the term is defined in Chapter 1 as the resultant of a complex series of processes and flows. At the risk of using a currently overworked term, one must utilize the "systems approach" or "system view" to gain an operationally useful understanding of the labor market and its participants. Essentially, the purpose of the systems approach is to identify the various elements in a process, clarify their functions, and trace their interrelationships.

First, each element of the system can be considered in the context of the process as a whole. The inputs into that element and its outputs, as traced in the system's description, provide continuity.

Interrelationships, dependencies, and constraints with other elements of the system are not lost track of when any single piece is isolated for analysis.

Secondly, the systems approach provides an extremely useful multiplicity of focus. Since all systems are seen as made up of subsystems, any "box" in the system's representation may be opened up into a series of subsystems (smaller boxes and their interrelationships) by narrowing the analyst's focus, and conversely several boxes may be enclosed in a larger system. For example, in a subsequent illustration of the employment system, we identify "employer facilities" as a component or "box" in the diagram. A researcher interested in opening up this box could elaborate it into a series of functional subsystems consisting of, say, production, accounting, engineering, etc. Each of these in turn could be further subdivided into individual job descriptions or even a series of work elements or ultimately hand motions themselves.

Finally, the systems approach permits the analyst to ignore the inner workings of some elements in the system without losing the continuity of the flows and interrelationships of the total process. One can always treat an element in the system as a "black box;" one notes its position in the system, its inputs and outputs to other elements, without looking inside it to understand how it achieves the transforms that it does.

For example, in our system's representation we identify an element labeled "vocational training." It will be treated as a "black box" in our subsequent discussion. Vocational training is not examined in detail, yet its position in the flow process is noted, as are its relationships to the job market and higher education, two elements that are selected for more detailed examination.*

In this work we intend to make full use of these advantages. We will first lay out the over-all system, identifying the major elements and their relationships. In subsequent chapters we will open up several boxes for closer examination of the subsystems within them. We will treat others as "black boxes," since several of them are examined in detail in other studies currently sponsored by the Department of Labor.

## AN OVER-ALL VIEW OF THE SYSTEM

The conceptual framework for this volume is one that visualizes "job market," as traditionally thought of, as the central element in a system of manpower on the one side and employment on the other. From the manpower side of the system "prospective employees" flow into (and out of) the job market element, while "job vacancies" flow into (and out of) it from the employment side. A simple representation of only the direct flow elements of the system is pictured in Figure 2.1; we shall later introduce several intermediaries that affect this flow.

On the right, or manpower, side of the diagram, we begin with the national population or family. The flow of prospective employees originates there and essentially without exception proceeds through primary education. This is the elementary school system through which virtually every member of the U.S. work force has gone. Beyond this point several alternate routes are available. "Vocational education" embraces those public or private schools that provide a commercial or vocational training for their students. "Higher education" encompasses a variety of academic and professional facilities. In some cases higher education includes some form of professional apprenticeship or internship experience. "Skills training" refers to a variety of training courses or programs specializing in specific occupational skill development. Courses in

---

*A current Conservation of Human Resources Study on the relationship of labor market information to metropolitan labor markets will include an analysis of the role of labor market information in determining the occupational skills taught in the New York City public vocational high schools.

20

FIGURE 2.1

The Labor Market: Direct Flows System

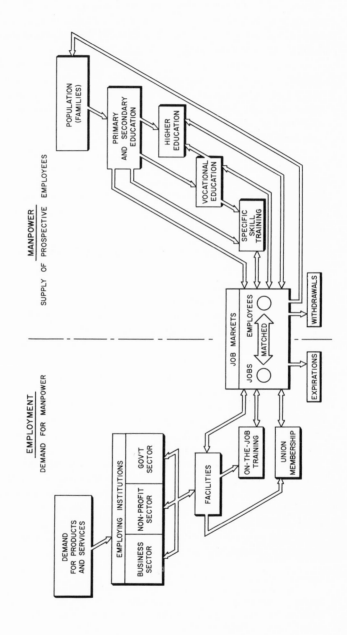

computer programing, arc welding, or the duties of hospital orderlies are typical examples of skill training.

As can be seen by the diagramed arrows, flows from primary and secondary education to the labor market may pass through one, several, or none of these intermediate steps. Equally important are the flows in the opposite direction. People leave the job market, headed back to any of the elements we noted, or "drop out" via retirement, marriage, sickness, or death. The process is dynamic and continuous. Two-way flows occur at any given moment. The notion of an equilibrium in this system is difficult to conceptualize.

On the left, or employment, side of our diagram, we attempt to trace the flow of "job vacancies" into the job market. While the concept is less tangible, and rather more slippery than "people," one can still logically trace the creation of "job vacancies." Starting with the broad notion of demand for goods and services (both private and public), we identify a series of "institutions" for providing them. We categorize such institutions in three broad classifications: the business sector, the nonprofit sector, and the government sector. Such classification is primarily useful in view of the fact that there have been dramatic changes in the relative sizes and rates of growth of these sectors in recent decades.

The institutions provide and maintain a range of "facilities" or physical locations for housing jobs and job vacancies. The facilities, in effect, structure and define job and job vacancies as to physical location and functional and occupational characteristics, as well as numerical size. Thus the facilities "deliver" to the job market the job vacancies we have been tracing. It is perhaps convenient to note that in some cases the job vacancy is delivered directly by the facility. In others an intermediate step of "on-the-job training" provided by the facility in reality creates the job vacancy. That is to say, there is a (job) vacancy for a trainee for a facility job rather than for the facility job itself.

It should be noted that job vacancies appearing on the job market are a result of the "netting out" of an employer's internal supply and demand for labor. A job vacancy may lead to a number of internal shifts or promotions, with the externally listed vacancy as their net result. Similarly, on-the-job training occurs as a prerequisite for many internal shifts and promotions, as well as an interface between the facility and the external job market. In this chapter, the internal job market is treated as a "black box" but is considered in more detail in Chapter 5.

Similarly, some job vacancies may be created through the intermediate step of "union membership." In these instances, union membership is a mandatory condition, sometimes before, sometimes after employment; the job vacancy, therefore, exists for a membership in the facility's union. The same consideration would apply for job vacancies requiring membership in other professional associations or, to some extent, those requiring some form of licensing, apprenticeship, certification, or academic degree.

Once again note should be taken of the reverse flows indicated in the diagram. Job vacancies are both created and destroyed. Not only can a vacancy be eliminated by matching it with a potential employee, but it can also be withdrawn without being filled. A variety of causes including obsolescence may remove job vacancies temporarily or more permanently. Similarly many vacancies may be significantly altered in nature or scope, as a result of changed demands or perceived supply. These are probably best viewed as withdrawals and substitutions by other job vacancies.

On a larger scale, facilities are similarly subject to creation and destruction. They may be closed down, temporarily or permanently, moved, or modified in function. The impacts of such changes on the job vacancies that they deliver to the labor market is obvious. In an even broader framework the institutions (the business, nonprofit, and governmental sectors) behind the facilities are constantly changing. While not many observers will argue for the foreseeable total elimination of one of the three institutional categories we cited, they are still subject to considerable flux. Individual organizations and agencies are continuously emerging and disappearing within each sector, while many functions and missions shift between sectors or call for an overlapping of two or three of them.

Thus on this side of the job market also, we find a complex and dynamic system, whose fluctuations have direct impact on the market. Again, it is a continuous, two-way flow of job vacancies, every bit as complex as the flow of people on the manpower side.[1]  In our diagram, then, the job market represents the confluence of two complex, dynamic streams, in which "prospective employees" arriving from one side are to be coupled with "job vacancies" arriving from the other. To add to the complexity of the process, it must be realized that the two inflows and outflows are not independent of each other nor of the larger economic system of which employment and manpower are a part.

This is perhaps a convenient place to note that the "systems approach" is not limited to dividing up a system, such as the manpower-employment one we are examining, into its subsystems. It is an equally useful approach in viewing the focal system itself as a subsystem of a higher-level, more comprehensive system, and thus subject to many forces and impacts: economic, political, and social, external to manpower and employment considerations *per se*. The level of economic activity, technological change, balance of payments, even changes in tastes, fashions, and styles may have profound impacts not reflected or reported in information generally classified as "manpower and employment" information. This means, quite simply, that regardless of how complete or comprehensive a "labor market information system" might be, policy-planners must be responsive to a large variety of "nonlabor market" information sources and trends. In many instances these will, in fact, prove to be far more crucial than the conventional "labor market" information sources. An assumption that even an ideal labor market information system will furnish the complete information required for policy formulation implies a closed-systems view, far removed from reality.

The box marked "job market" in our system's diagram will be opened up and examined in greater detail in Chapter 4. The overview of the system within which it is located, as presented here, should serve to underline the dangers inherent in dealing with the job market as either an isolated or a static phenomenon. While one can see intuitively that the job market is neither, our traditional concepts and record-keeping practices tend to shape our thinking in these directions. Many operational programs tend to visualize the job market as an exercise in matching a relatively static labor force with a given number of job vacancies. These often tend to ignore the complexities of a continuously changing size and mix of the two elements of the matchmaking efforts and their interdependence.

Even with a broader view of the system presented here we are often hampered by the nature of the data available. Our record keeping is, of necessity, largely restricted to instantaneous "snapshots" of the system. We are aware of numbers of people and jobs (or job vacancies) at different stages of the process and in rather coarse aggregates of demographic, regional, and occupational characteristics. We typically know less about the flows between stages. Individuals spotted at any stage may be moving along any one of the several routes we traced in the system, and they may be moving in either direction.

Attempts at estimating flows by measuring changes in levels are also subject to considerable distortion. In many instances flows are "netted out," thus masking the cross currents that result in the net flow. In many cases, the computed flows are those noted between the discrete time points at which levels are measured. As a result, a considerable amount of activity, occurring between measured time periods, may go completely unrecorded.[2] The number of actual "transactions" consummated in the labor market at any given time is grossly underestimated in our normal recording practices.

It is as well to note that the classifications we commonly use for aggregating data, for both levels and flows, can be quite imprecise, overlapping, and inconsistent.

Some classifications are determined quite subjectively by either the counted person or by his counter,while others may change their meaning over time and thus be inconsistent in longitudinal comparisons. These points are raised not as a critique of statistical methodology but rather to emphasize those factors in our data collection that serve to muddy our concept of the labor market. The point is simply that distorted, mechanical, and oversimplified data tend to lead us to a distorted, mechanical, oversimplified concept of reality.

Perhaps the most damaging flaw of an isolated view of the job market is its tendency to restrict our efforts at corrective actions to a single element in a large, interdependent system. Too narrow a focus on the "job market" box of the system implies that tinkering with its inner workings is the only way to cope with problems of manpower and employment. If unemployment rates are too high, rates of growth too low, or manpower supplies unbalanced, we tend to jump to the conclusion that some manipulation of the job market —

narrowly defined — is the only way to bring about correction. Thus, when information is the focus of attention, as it is in the present study, the tendency is to direct all attention at the information flows within the job market box. The implication is that great benefits will result from the improvement of information flows inside the market: more specifically the information needs of job hunters and employers looking for manpower. This view ignores the information needs of the system as a whole. More importantly it neglects the possibility that improving the information flows in other parts of the system may well yield payoffs far more significant than those associated with improved intramarket flows. For example, the recent size and severity of unemployment in the aerospace industry would have been more effectively alleviated by improved demand-forecasting and phasing out of major contracts than by supplying longer lists of employment opportunities to job seekers who had already been laid off.

This narrow-focus view can perhaps be best illustrated by analogy to the more familiar market for consumer products. It would be equivalent to the manufacturer of, say, soap restricting his total market effort to improved point-of-sale promotion and ignoring any market research on buyer needs and tastes, product development and modification, competitors' responses, mass media advertising, and problems of distribution and pricing. His total effort would be concentrated on presenting better or more immediate information about his product to the shopper examining the soap shelf in the supermarket. While such additional information would probably result in some increase in sales, it is highly probable that the same expenditure of money and effort in other parts of the system — in front of, and behind, the supermarket shelf — would yield far more impressive growth in sales and a better response to the changing character of tastes and technology, in the long run far more important to the company than tomorrow's sales.

A final word of caution need be sounded in interpreting the system pictured in Figure 2.1. It, quite obviously, does not assume a single, homogeneous job market for the nation. It is merely a graphic representation of a multitude of job markets that exist along several dimensions. Most markets can be segregated geographically; many others may be classified by occupation, profession, or industry. Many of these overlap. We simply mention this obvious fact to avoid the impression of a monolithic, tightly linked system that, by implication, must rely on a centralized, tightly integrated, and articulated information system. Such a conception of a labor market information system is technically and economically unfeasible and is doomed to failure.

## INTERMEDIARIES AND THEIR ROLES IN THE SYSTEM

Our conceptual framework has, so far, dealt with actions of primary participants in the labor market: prospective employees and employers. We must now introduce a number of other forces that determine or influence the actions of these primary participants.

**FIGURE 2.2**

**Intermediaries: In Job/Man Matching**

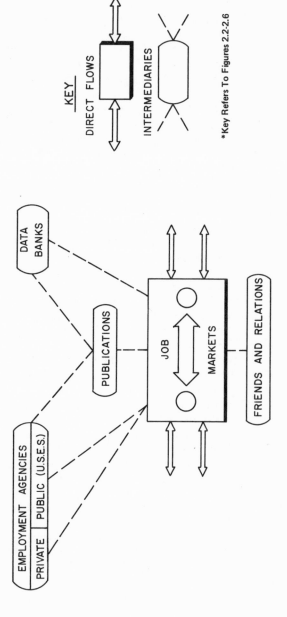

## Intermediaries

Several intermediaries participate in or exert their influence *directly* on the "job market." These are agencies or functions directly associated with matching prospective employees and job vacancies. They are shown superimposed over the central element of our system in Figure 2.2

From all that is known about the operation of the job market, friends and relations appear to be much the most commonly used sources of information for job seekers in the market. Clearly this category embodies a shifting, indistinct, and widely diverse consistency. Its information is highly segmented, usually quite limited in scope for any individual job seeker, and undoubtedly contains major errors and gaps. On the other hand it can be extremely rich in detail and "flavor." Our subsequent discussion of information characteristics will indicate that, although highly informal, this kind of data is uniquely tailored to the needs of job seekers and employers.

A more formal set of intermediaries is represented by the boxes marked "employment agencies" and "data banks." The former is divided into private, nonprofit, and public — the last-named largely the United States Employment Service (USES). "Agencies" are very diverse in size, function, and ownership. Private agencies, for example, overwhelmingly tend to specialize by occupational classification and industry. Publicly sponsored "data banks," on the other hand, relative newcomers to the field, essentially attempt to provide nonspecialized services to assist agencies in mechanical job matching and may be directly associated with them.

In addition to their direct influence on job transactions through personal contact with the primary participants, agencies and data banks may influence the flow of job seekers and job opportunities through a variety of published information sources. Shown as "publications" in Figure 2.2, these cover a wide range: from mass circulation media to proprietary newsletters; association listings, and private mailings.

This study will not examine any of these intermediaries in detail, since they form the focal point of several other studies in the Department of Labor's current research effort.

Employment agency and USES roles are examined in detail in the Bay State Area study conducted by Margaret Thal-Larsen.[3] Job matching through computerized data banks is being studied by George P. Huber and Joseph C. Ullman[4] in extensive projects sponsored by the Department of Labor. In addition, a number of other studies and pilot-plant installations are being operated throughout the country.

### Indirect Intermediaries: Manpower Side

We can now move to other intermediaries whose impact is directed at something other than the central element of our system. Moving to the manpower side of our model, we will deal with two intermediaries in the manpower education and training components. These are illustrated as "guidance" and "curriculum planning" in Figure 2.3. They have an impact, of

# FIGURE 2.3

## Intermediaries: In Manpower Development

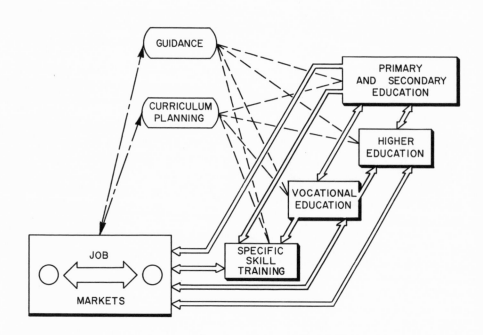

varying intensity, on all stages of the education and training process. Let us briefly consider their respective functions.

"Guidance" is the generic term applied to the function that assists and helps shape the occupational and career choices of prospective employees arriving at the job market. It helps an individual select the route by which he arrives, and it also focuses the search and defines the expectations of the arrival. In both these terms the guidance function has an important bearing on the job market. The selection of routes determines the qualitative content of the unit we have been calling "prospective employees," as well as the lead time (or delay) in arrival at the market. The shaping of expectations and self-definition of the prospective employee largely determines the specific job market he will consider relevant in his search for a job vacancy. It is in this area that guidance can play a crucial role.

"Curriculum Planning" is used as a broad term for defining those functions that determine the kinds of training and education that will be provided at each stage in the manpower development process. It determines the goals and missions, the appropriate population and prerequisites, the course content and pedagogy, as well as the performance and achievement levels of the program's output. Clearly other than labor market considerations enter the curriculum planning effort. Its importance, however, must not be short-changed. Consideration of life-styles, value systems, and attitudes to work (all labor market-related issues) enter into the curriculum planning of elementary schools as well as the most esoteric of nonprofessional, liberal arts colleges. In any event, our concern here is focused on those aspects of curriculum planning most directly responsive to the demands of the job market.

As in the case of guidance, curriculum planning helps determine the quality of the prospective employee arriving at the job market, as well as shaping his expectations. To a much larger extent than guidance, this phase also has significant impacts on the shaping of job vacancies arriving at the other end of the labor market. Educational norms in many instances, most strikingly in the professions, often define an occupation or a job vacancy. The structuring of an accountant's, a civil engineer's, or even a secretary's job in an employer's facility is largely determined by the curriculum definition given these occupations at the training facility. While the two elements are interdependent, at least in the short-run, employers define many of their job vacancies in terms of the products of educational and training curriculums.

In this study, we focus our attention on the curriculum-planning function in higher education, more specifically at the college and university level. We make this choice for a number of reasons. Curriculum planning of special skills programs has already received wide attention, particularly in connection with the many programs associated with the Manpower Development and Training Act. Furthermore, the connection between such planning and the needs of the labor market is so obvious as not to require elaboration. The same is true of vocational education. The central role of labor market needs in their curriculum planning cannot escape the primary attention of its many planners. By contrast, higher education has been made much more insulated from its relations with the labor market. Coupled with a certain amount of tradition

# FIGURE 2.4

## Intermediaries: In Employment Planning

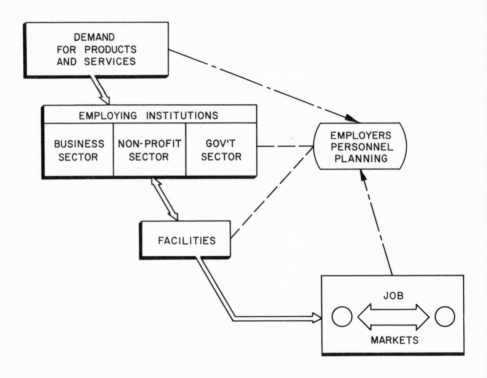

and perhaps academic pride, this insularity has tended to make response often sluggish and, occasionally, almost totally absent. Our study of this stage of curriculum planning should be useful in improving the responsiveness of education to the total system's needs at a time when the role of higher education as a whole is being questioned. Finally, our research team has particular competence in this area. Equally important, it has realistic humility in resisting the temptation to plunge into the subject of curriculum planning in primary education.

### Indirect Intermediaries: Employment Side

Moving over to the employment side of the system, we identify the primary intermediary here as the function of "employers' personnel planning." (see Figure 2.4) This is an admittedly broad classification encompassing a large variety of activities and institutional settings. Such planning is done at the institutional and facility level and with varying degrees of formality. Personnel planning is viewed as the process that determines a facility's current and future manpower needs. It specifies the numbers, types, and locations of both jobs and job vacancies in the organization and thus serves as the major guideline for hiring, promoting, and transferring, and laying off. Personnel planning can be short-or long-run. Short-run planning determines current creation (or destruction) of "job vacancies." Longer-run planning may have some secondary impacts on current job vacancies, but its major influence will be felt in future demands on the labor market. It shapes the future flow of job vacancies to the market by determining the types of facilities and processes to be used, their location, and their manpower needs. Such planning may have lead times ranging from a few months to several years. The extreme is reached in the case of universities and the civil service, where tenure may commit labor decisions for years to come, even decades.

Personnel planning, as we have used the term here, is obviously related to many other of the employer's planning activities and to his interpretation of environmental trends. The employer's perception of his mission and strategy, his current resources and opportunities, the state of technological advance in his field, are only a few of the factors that affect personnel planning. Sometimes these are consciously and systematically considered, and a formal manpower plan is developed. At other times no conscious plan is formulated, but operating decisions are taken as alternatives present themselves. These decisions, by determining, say, the location and size of new facilities, inevitably shape the demand for manpower, hence the flow of "job vacancies" to the market. We, therefore, identify "employers' personnel planning" as an important intermediary in our system, whether such planning is formally carried out by the employer or not.

Personnel planning, in broad terms, has been an important employer activity for a long time and is likely to grow in importance in the years ahead. A considerable amount of research, knowledge, and literature have been amassed in this area. It is obviously not our intent, in this study, to examine the full scope of this activity. In Chapter 5, we focus our attention on the personnel planning function as it relates to the informational needs and uses of the large private employer.

## Indirect Intermediaries: Over-All System Impact

We are now ready to turn our attention to two important intermediaries whose impact spans a broad range of the system. They exert influence on the job market itself, as well as both manpower and employment policy on either side of it. They are broadly termed "unions" and "government policy" in our framework. Both intermediaries, obviously, perform a wide range of social and political functions. Equally obviously, our concern with them here is primarily, but not entirely, limited to the influences they exert on shaping the "prospective employee," on the one hand, and the "job vacancy," on the other.

"Unions" broadly refers to organized labor in its many forms. On the manpower side of our system, unions, particularly craft unions, have important impacts on the level and quality of skills training and vocational education. They may help prescribe the acceptable performance and achievement levels and thus, indirectly, effect curriculum planning and pedagogy. They may be highly influential in the setting of occupational competence definition and in licensing or certifying trade acceptance. They are also an important factor in the shaping of expectations and, hence, the career choices of prospective employees. Unions, then, have an impact on several stages of the manpower system and are one of the important forces determining the numbers, quality, and timing of arrivals at the job market, both directly and through their effect on wage levels.

On the employment side, unions are often instrumental in shaping the "job vacancy" that appears on the market. They may set the constraints within which employer hiring is carried out, spell out the job description to be performed, or determine which job vacancies are to be assigned to the job market as against being filled from within. We have already noted in our basic system layout the role that union membership serves in the direct flow of job vacancies to the market. All these are examples of the direct and immediate influence of the unions on job vacancies.

Unions, both industrial and craft, also exert considerable indirect and longer-range influence on the labor market. Collective bargaining, work rules, and wage rates are but a few examples of the facts that influence employers' personnel planning. They thus help shape employers' facility planning, manpower needs, and constraints. Employers' decisions on facility location, technology exploitation, and process selection may be significantly guided by union policy and practice. To this extent the numbers, types, and timing of future job vacancies appearing on the labor market are subject to union influence.

Finally, unions have a direct impact on the job market itself. In some instances the union provides the actual framework of the market, as in the case of hiring halls. In others it functions in a manner similar to the employment agency and could well be visualized as occupying that box in Figure 2.2. In many other instances, union agreements or policies provide the constraints (of wage rates or occupational definitions) within which "prospective employees"

32

FIGURE 2.5

Intermediaries: Unions

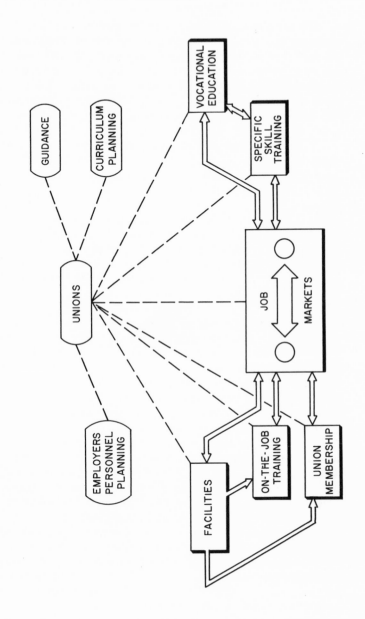

and "job vacancies" are matched or within which the match may be bargained.

We have not attempted to examine in any detail in this volume the many and important aspects of union activities that bear on the flow of information within job markets or the labor market as a whole. So important, however, and in our view somewhat neglected, are these activities that among our recommendations for further study is a full-fledged program of research in this area. Of particular importance in our opinion is an examination of the role of unions in the informational process that influences transactions in the internal labor market of large-scale employers. In this chapter we simply identify the union and its primary functions in the system. Figure 2.5 diagrams union and union-like bodies (for example, the American Medical Association and the American Association of University Professors) in our system. The final intermediary to be discussed, government at all levels, is the most pervasive of all. Its influence is felt at every stage of our system. Its impact is sometimes direct: as designing, financing, and operating special skills training programs under the Manpower Development and Training Act. Or its influence can be highly indirect, through its actions in the larger socio-economic system, as in formulating fiscal policies that affect the rates of growth of demand, facility expansion or contraction, and over-all strategies of employer institutions. It seems hardly necessary to check off, point by point, the impacts of government policy on each stage of the system we have defined. It is sufficient to identify two major classes of government policy: "economic policy" *per se* and the economic effects of other policies, which have major if indirect impact on the shaping of job vacancies arriving at the job market; and "education and manpower policy," which affects more directly the flow of prospective employees to the market.

Government policy is formulated at a variety of levels. "Federal, state, and local" as one way of sorting it out, but not the only way. It can be equally well separated by national, regional, or local segments within the three political subdivisions. It can, further, be focused on specific industries, types of manpower, or segments of the population. The scope and range of this function are enormous. We will restrict our attention to the federal government and its broader policy considerations. We believe that this is the area in which the greatest needs exist and the one that to a great degree shapes the formulation of policy at other levels. To some extent what we say about the federal government's needs for information will be found applicable to other levels also. Our approach, then, can be treated as a pilot study for closer examination of other governmental entities and their influence on the labor market. One of our specific recommendations, in fact, focuses primarily on a pilot study of local labor market information systems.

## CONCLUSIONS

In this chapter we presented, first, a model of the labor market that visualizes a "job market" as a central element in a relatively simple system. The system traces the flows of the two main components with which the market deals: "prospective employees" and "job vacancies." We have intentionally steered clear from such commonly used, but definitionally slippery, terms as "labor force," "vacancy listing," "unemployment rates," or "chronically unemployed." All these can be explained as variously defined measurements of stocks and flows of the two major components of our framework. We did, however, point up the variety and importance of the flows through the system. We noted the dangers inherent in focusing total attention on the central element of the system solely, or of treating it as a tightly linked, monolithic structure.

We then proceeded to identify the roles and impacts of several critical intermediaries in the system. These are critical in the sense that their actions significantly modify the flows and arrivals of the two main inputs into the job market. They affect rates of flows in and out, routes of flow, as well as the qualitative characteristics of both inputs. We identified intermediaries in a number of categories: (1) those that impact directly on the market (friends and relations, employment agencies, and data banks); (2) those that influence primarily the manpower side of the system (guidance and curriculum planning); (3) those that influence the employment side (employers' planning); (4) finally those that affect the entire range of the system (unions and government policy). Figure 2.6 shows all intermediaries discussed superimposed over the basic flow system.

The resultant diagram is perhaps confusingly cluttered, but it serves to highlight our earlier discussion of the complexity of the systems we are examining and the broad range of interdependencies in its functioning. It also, we hope, emphasizes the inadequacy of seeking improvement on information flows solely *inside* the job market. Improved performance by the intermediaries, through better information, might well have a more significant impact on the effectiveness of the labor market than would enlarging the information inputs to job seekers and employers directly. We, further, drew attention to the fact that even the complex diagram we present here is only a subsystem of a large socioeconomic system that often produces major external impacts on the structure of employment and manpower.

One other aspect of our system diagram (Figure 2.6) should be noted at this point. The information needs of the elements plotted are somewhat related to their location in the diagram space. The horizontal dimension relates to the time horizon of the information needed; the vertical dimension corresponds to the degree of detail. Thus, along the horizontal dimension, the center of our diagram, where the job market is positioned, represents need for *current* information. We essentially need to know which job vacancies and prospective employees exist today. As we move outward, to either side, we become concerned with progressively longer time horizons and, in effect, deal with longer-term forecasts. Thus "specific skill training," on the one side, and "on-the-job training" on the other, are made in response to relatively short-range forecasts of market demand and supply. On the other hand, "primary and secondary education" and "institutions" must be concerned with comparatively long-range forecasts of the market.

Along the vertical dimension, we can roughly range information needs as being highly detailed at the bottom of the diagram and largely aggregative at

# FIGURE 2.6

## Overall System: Direct Flows and Intermediaries

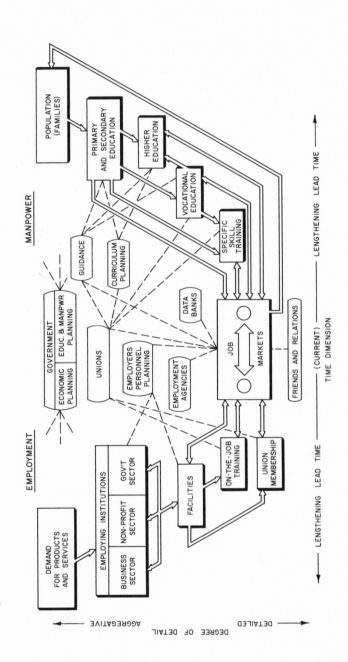

36

the top. Direct participants in the labor market need to know considerable details about specific job vacancies, for example, while higher education curriculum planning or government economic policy decisions are based on large aggregates, summaries, and consolidations of data.

With the over-all system as background, we can proceed to open up some of the boxes for closer examination, including our central element: the job market itself. These examinations will constitute Part II of this volume. Before proceeding to these specifics, we need to examine one more element of our conceptual framework: a generalized view of information and information systems. This is done in Chapter 3.

# 3

# INFORMATION
# AND COMPREHENSIVE
# INFORMATION SYSTEMS

The Department of Labor has been charged with maintaining not merely an information system about the labor market, but a "comprehensive" information system. To get some sense of what "comprehensive" might mean, it is perhaps best to review briefly some fundamental notions of information and information systems.

## THE RANGE AND RICHNESS OF INFORMATION

If one begins to think about the full nature or range of information used by decision-makers, one is immediately struck by its enormous richness and variety. Quantitative, numerical, or "hard" data are easiest to process and manipulate but are only a small portion of the total range of information. A much broader layer is represented by qualitative and descriptive data deriving from written, verbal, even sensory sources. Numerical data lend themselves to convenient storing and aggregating, are often more objective, and may provide the decision-maker with a clear-cut method of comparing and evaluating alternatives. On the other hand, the fact that qualitative data are difficult to assemble and disseminate does not make them any less relevant or important.

## USERS AND USES OF INFORMATION

In discussing the richness and variety of information, we referred to decision-makers several times. This is a point that needs to be made quite explicit. The gathering and processing of information always incurs costs. For this information to have a value, it must serve some purpose. Tightly defined (in dealing with "value of information" in Decision Theory), information has value only when it causes the decision-maker to take a *different* course of action from the one he would have selected without it. If a somewhat less rigid definition is accepted, information has value if it improves the quality of any decision or even increases the confidence of the decision-maker in his choice. It becomes obvious then, that one cannot discuss the value of information without a clear indentification of the decision-maker using it and the decision for which it is used. In other words, there can be no meaningful examination of information without explicit indentification of *user* and *use*.

In these terms the task of developing a comprehensive labor market information system is a formidable one. There are literally millions of direct participants in the market (users) facing an almost infinite set of decisions (uses). Obviously the system designer must proceed to classify users and uses to arrive at a manageable conceptual framework. A practical simplification (similar to that used in the Weber report[1]) is to impose on a labor market information system the groupings we identify as the major blocks in our systems view of Chapter 2: that is, to deal in terms of the information needs of the primary or direct participants — employers and employees (actual and potential) — on the one hand, and with the various intermediaries — the manpower program administrators, policy-makers, and planners (at the federal, state, regional, and local levels), guidance counselors and interviewers, educational and training institutions, unions and professional societies, and public and private employment agencies — forming another grouping as secondary participants. These intermediaries, as we have argued, may have a greater cumulative impact on the labor market and its trends than the direct participants. The wide range of problems they must deal with places correspondingly greater demands on the labor market information system.

## THE CHARACTERISTICS OF INFORMATION

The identification of users and uses, then, is the first step in determining what information is needed in the system. It is well to note at the outset that all information has a time dimension and collected data almost invariably deal with the past. Several important and frequently overlapping characteristics of past data need to be noted here: accuracy (broadly defined to include reliability, consistency, and comparability), detail, timeliness, and frequency. Each is briefly discussed, as it applies to some of the major existing information sources on labor markets.

### Accuracy, Consistency, and Comparability

The history of data collection in the United States, particularly at the national level, has been marked by a constant striving for accuracy and heroic efforts to overcome the intransigence of the data. Where significant inaccuracy occurs, as in the undercounting of minority groups in the census, the responsible agency is usually well aware of the problem and, where possible, attempts rectification.

The accuracy and reliability of data depends on many factors including the methods of collection, extent of coverage, consistency and comparability over time and across sources, statistical methodologies employed, processing techniques, and, increasingly, the ability to enlist the cooperation of data-supplying groups. It is, therefore, not surprising that slippage on any of these counts remains an ever present possibility. Furthermore, efforts to improve accuracy by adding data sources or expanding coverage often lead to new problems of incompatibility or noncomparability across data sources. Thus, for example, the establishment reporting method that is based on a count of jobs rather than job holders cannot give an accurate estimate of that part of the labor force that is employed. The household visitation sampling method of collecting data for the Current Population Survey (CPS), which concentrates on the job holder rather than the job, avoids the double-counting involved in establishment reporting.

Another example is furnished by the differences in measurements of unemployment that are derived from the CPS on the one hand and from the administrative records on unemployment insurance on the other. The latter data are drawn from the total universe of unemployment insurance claims, rather than a sample. There are, however, numerous exclusions from unemployment insurance coverage (of those not legally covered, of those who have exhausted their benefits, etc.), with those excluded groups later being "factored in" to arrive at a total estimate of unemployment. Such restricted coverage makes more reliable and meaningful the CPS measure with its operational definition of the unemployed as all those who were not working during the survey week but were looking for work, regardless of whether or not they were eligible for unemployment insurance.

Similarly, at the state and local levels widespread statutory and administrative variations in coverage and definition (of partial and total unemployment, for example) almost guarantee a lack of comparability between states and regions and within the same state over time. Thus employment is usually counted at place of employment while unemployment may be counted at place of residence, of prior employment, or of claim, rendering interarea comparisons almost meaningless. Further, the accuracy of employment estimates in smaller and rural areas is frequently suspect.

The history of occupational statistics provides an unfortunately rich source of examples of the inaccuracy associated with inconsistency in basic definitions and a lack of standard classifications over time, place, and data sources. The fewer than 300 occupational classes used by the census, with one-third of the work performed in the U.S. economy lumped in the "nec" ("not elsewhere classified") category are not only inadequate but are also not strictly comparable with Bureau of Labor Statistics (BLS), Dictionary of Occupational Titles (DOT), and industry classifications. In this case the household visitation method of collecting data is inferior to establishment reporting, whose use was recommended in the Gordon report.[2]

### Detail

One way of enhancing accuracy as well as permitting finer, multipurpose analysis is to provide sufficient and meaningful detail. Referring again to occupational statistics of the census, many of the classes at the one-digit level reflect a spurious aggregation of superficially similar occupations (stockbrokers and newsboys both included in the "sales" category). Too broad definitions prevent the demarcation of truly homogeneous jobs; operationally meaningful definitions require sufficient detail. The initiation of the new federal-state occupational employment statistics program,[3] which will utilize mail question-naire surveys of employment by occupation, is a big step in the development of employment definitions with adequate detail. These definitions are broadly similar to those used by the census but are far more detailed at the individual occupational level and are compatible with DOT titles.

At this point, it may be well to point out that "more accurate" (or more detailed) information is not *ipso facto* "better" information. Not only does added accuracy and detail involve greater costs, but many needs of decision-makers call only for rough approximations where the cost of further refine-ment cannot be justified in terms of improved decisions. The determination of which supplemental questions may be added to the CPS sample is but one example of the many areas in which such a balancing of costs and benefits is required.

Another dimension of cost should be remembered as well — the cost in lost accuracy that can be expected where any data-supplying group feels resentful of the demands imposed by the data collectors and sees no benefits, even indirect ones. Compliance is then secured by legislation, but, as in the case of Equal Employment Opportunity Commission compliance, we can expect to find a mix of "manufactured" and real data.

On the other hand, there are situations where even a substantial increase in money costs would be warranted because of the significantly greater benefits in accuracy that would accrue. The Emergency Employment Act of 1971 makes available substantial sums to state and local governments, the amounts dependent on state unemployment security agency estimates of the extent of area unemployment. The inherent limitations on the accuracy of such estimates to which we have referred before might well justify an acceptance of a different method of collecting such data, such as the CPS household visitation method, greatly expanded in sample size, despite the significantly higher cost involved. Another alternative, lower in direct cost but perhaps more difficult to achieve, is getting more accurate, voluntarily supplied data by giving the supplier a *quid pro quo* in terms of more usable information for his specific needs. This approach is explored in our recommendation for local labor market informa-tion systems in Chapter 9.

### Timeliness and Frequency of Information

There is an inevitable time lag ranging from hours to years between the observation of labor market events and their recording, analysis, and dissemina-tion. Delays may be inherent in the method of collection or the extent of processing, or may simply be a matter of priority in allocating limited resources. The decay over time in the value of past information can only be combated by periodic updating. The length of the updating cycle (always highly variable) determines the frequency with which information is available. Data may be updated on a daily or weekly basis, or every decade as in the case of the full census. An extreme case is the one-time or special-purpose survey. There is no prescribed frequency for this sort of information, which is in fact obtained on demand.

The date of release of data is frequently crucial. Almost instantaneous publication is essential to the operation of the Job Bank. On the other hand, census data are sometimes used (frequently on a "lack of better" basis) almost a decade after publication. Lack of timeliness can, in some cases, vitiate the accuracy of the results — the fact that state employment figures are reported quarterly but are often, because of processing delays, not available for several months, makes them unusable as current labor force estimates. The importance of timeliness depends on where on the time axis one is operating — the macro-planner is frequently not under the same pressures as one closer to the heat of day-to-day decision-making, and for him improving the timeliness of statistics is usually not nearly so important.

We are reminded by S.A. Goldberg and C.C. Hodgins, of the Dominion Bureau of Statistics in Ottawa, that,

> While promptness enhances the value of statistics, often immeasurably, reliable data which are late in coming are nonetheless useful for current analysis . . . good decisions are not, or should not, be based only on the latest figures but on a set of expectations about the evolving situation. A solid view on the outlook can be established only by an analysis of the historical record, extending over many months or years. Thus, the frequently quoted assertion that timeliness is important because "statistical information is a highly perishable commodity" is an oversimplification.[4]

## INFORMATION FOR PLANNING AND INFORMATION FOR CONTROL

Conceptually, at least, every user and every use may call for differing mixes of the characteristics of information enumerated above. Conceptual simplification is achieved by classifying the various uses of information by the two principal managerial functions: planning and control. Planning, similar to the common usage of the word, refers to the setting of objectives and designing programs and projects for their achievement. Control, in the managerial sense, deals with the broader issues of appraising and evaluating performance, not simply verifying the accuracy of reports. It attempts to measure the extent to which goals and objectives were met, compares actual performance against standards established in planning, and determines whether corrective action is called for. Since control focuses on what has already been done, its information needs are past oriented or historical. Planning, by contrast, is concerned with the future, and planning decisions are based primarily on explicit or implicit projections from the historical record.

## Information for Planning

The planner needs to see the environment as a whole, discern long-term trends, and perceive interdependencies among various programs and events. In terms of the information characteristics we outlined, one would expect planning to have the following characteristics:

(1) There is a relatively low degree of detail — aggregates, summations, and large classifications are usually more meaningful and easier to deal with.

(2) Timeliness is generally not crucial. There is an implicit lead time in all planning, and conversely one determinant of the required lead time is the availability of the needed data.

(3) For similar reasons, as long as available data are frequent enough to project future trends, the filling of intermediate time points generally contributes little to the longer-run forecasts.

(4) Pinpoint accuracy, as we have used the term, is not of critical importance. In many instances, predictive models are necessarily quite crude, and refinement of data is not likely to contribute significantly to the quality of the forecast. Moreover, since most important decisions must be made in a world of uncertainty and risk, realistic forecasting frequently takes the form of statements about probability distributions.

(5) Consistency and comparability are generally important in planning applications. Consistency over time is a prime ingredient in projecting future trends from past data, and, generally speaking, the longer the period over which data are available the better. Comparability and consistency between data series are also valuable. Since planning usually requires consideration of several programs or factors, the various departments and agencies involved must use comparable data if their plans are to be coordinated.

## Information for Control

Consider, in contrast, the information needs for control. Generally speaking, control must be exercised over specific programs or even subunits of programs. It must focus on relatively minor detail, in rather short periods of time, if the need for corrective action is to be identified clearly and promptly. In terms of the characteristics of information needs, consider the contrast to planning:

(1) A high degree of detail is essential. Since corrective action must be sharply focused, it is necessary to know where, by how much, and why performance did not match standard or goal. Aggregating of control information can often mask or distort the need for corrective action. A training program, for example, in which one class achieves results twice as good as anticipated while another only meets 50 percent of its goals would appear to be exactly on target if both class performance measures are aggregated. This information may be of some use in assessing the total effectiveness of the training program but is hardly sufficient for detecting the need for, or the application of, corrective action.

(2) Timeliness is often critical in control applications. If something has gone wrong, the sooner it is discovered and corrected, the better. If curriculum planning and manpower training programs are too late in responding to the signals transmitted by the job market, the result will be an endless series of delayed corrections and countercorrections. Such delayed responses, instead of bringing the system to equilibrium, often amplify the divergences and thus make the situation worse.

(3) Frequency of information is usually also a desirable feature in control applications. Monitoring relatively short time periods permits early identification of problems. Short periods of time imply a relatively high frequency of data availability.

(4) Accuracy, likewise, is required for control. Before embarking on corrective action or dispensing rewards, one would like to be as certain of the facts as possible.

(5) Consistency and comparability, on the other hand, play a relatively minor role. Control information, as we have seen, tends to span comparatively short time periods and generally focuses on single projects. Problems of comparability over time or across data sources tend to be minimized.

The rather striking differences in the characteristics of information for planning and control is evident. This dichotomy is, of course, neither pure nor universal, and in an efficient system the planning and control functions will interact in a continuing and reinforcing fashion. Thus Manpower Automated Reporting System (MARS) and Employment Security Automated Reporting System (ESARS) when fully operational should provide data on trainees in manpower programs and on applicants seeking employment security services including follow-up on placements. These systems should facilitate interaction between the planning and evaluation and control stages of manpower programs and point to corrective action where necessary.

We believe nevertheless that the rough distinction between planning and control is highly useful in sorting out the primary needs for information systems users. As we will show later, existing information on labor markets is far more useful for macro-level planning than for control uses. From the probes reported in Part II, the evidence is also clear that existing information sources all too often have limited utility for users at the micro and local levels either for planning or control purposes.

## DATA COLLECTION, ANALYSIS, AND INTERPRETATION

We can outline at this point the stages followed by decision-makers in obtaining and using information. Three distinct steps are involved: data are collected and stored; processed and assembled for analysis of a particular situation or for answering specific queries; and only then interpreted in terms of their implications for decision and action.

### Data Collection and Analysis

Traditionally, the statistical agencies of the government, particularly those charged with the development of labor market statistics, have seen their task as primarily the collection and orderly display of such data, usually in the form of statistical tables. (As we will show later, the bulk of existing labor market information is presented in such tables.) Although the statistical agencies might call attention to facets of these tables, it has not, by and large, been considered the proper province of the statistical agencies to carry out sophisticated analyses of the raw data.

Instead, private or public users of the data directly involved in the labor market are expected to know best how to use the data for their purposes while university personnel and research institutes are largely involved in the integration of theory and statistical data. With a few exceptions econometric studies of the labor market have been left to the universities and research institutes.

## Data Interpretation

Most policy- and decision-makers, both public and private, respond to *interpreted* data. Occasionally they will provide the interpretation themselves from analyzed data, but it is extremely rare for decision-makers to have the competence or time to develop an analysis from raw data.

A congressional committee, for example, typically arrives at conclusions from a series of *interpretations* of data presented to it by a variety of experts or interested parties or occasionally by its own staff. Often conflicting interpretations of the same raw data are presented, and committee deliberations proceed in effect along the adversary system. Decisions are presumably reached on the basis of judgments of the validity, consistency, or persuasiveness of the several interpretations presented. Much the same considerations apply to corporate executives, institutional planners, and university administrators.

## The State of the Art

The interpretation of data is likely to be a subjective, value-laden, and politically sensitive process, whereas data collection (once it has been decided what data are to be assembled) is relatively "neutral" and technical. In this sense the intermediate stage of data analysis falls somewhere between the two. While the choice of model, processing method, or even hypothesis selection will influence the results of the analysis, there are often relatively objective parameters on which technicians can agree. An obviously biased or slanted analysis can usually be recognized and rejected by informed observers. We are, therefore, prepared to treat the analysis stage as a reasonable extension of the data collection phase, which can be properly handled by agency technicians.

There have been several results of the division of labor between the statistician, primarily concerned with problems of collecting data and ensuring its reliability, and the theorist, interested in using data to test his hypothesis. Recently a distinguished theoretician and empirical investigator, Wassily Leontief, has called attention to some pernicious effects of the situation.[5] As he sees it, "The weak and *all too slowly growing empirical foundations* clearly cannot support the proliferating superstructure of pure, or should I say, speculative theory."

The gravity of the data inadequacies is compounded by the fact that the data of the social sciences are fundamentally different from those of the physical sciences. The social scientist studies a "system that is not only exceedingly complex, but is also in a state of constant flux."

> On the relatively shallow level where the empirically implemented economic analysis now operates even the more invariant of the structural relationships . . . change rapidly. Without a constant inflow of new data, the existing stock of factual information becomes obsolete very soon.

As Leontief sees it, the position of the social scientist is somewhat akin to that of Alice in a familiar part of Wonderland. "Just to keep up with our very modest current capabilities," he declares, "we have to maintain a steady flow of new data."

Further, it can be expected that information about labor markets, to be of use to national policy-makers and implementers, will have to be related more closely to broad major national goals and will therefore inevitably tend to transcend the old boundaries of labor market information. In the terminology of Chapter 2, complex as the labor market may be, it is only a subsystem of a far larger political and social system.

SOME PROBES
INTO SELECTED AREAS
OF LABOR MARKET
INFORMATION

# 4

## THE JOB MARKET: INFORMATIONAL AND POLICY IMPLICATIONS OF ITS STRUCTURE AND PROCESS

### INTRODUCTION

In Chapter 2 we sketched the "employment-manpower" system in its broad outlines and indicated some of the critical linkages in the system. It is across these that information must flow in order to integrate the actions taken by or within any of the subsystems with other subsystems of the "employment-manpower" system. One of these major linkages, a subsystem located on our general map of the labor market, is the set of job markets whose characteristics are detailed in Chapter 2. A primary characteristic of the set of job markets is that each of the indivudual job markets is uniquely located in many dimensions — e.g., by geographical area, occupation, industry, demographic characteristics, and so on. The arena circumscribed by the term the "job market" is thus extremely heterogeneous, and the decisions made by the various actors must be based on quite specific information concerning subsets of the job market.

### WHAT KIND OF MARKET IS THE LOCAL JOB MARKET?

Diversity and complexity characterize the various occupational-industrial matrixes that constitute the job market. In the *Dictionary of Occupational Titles* are listed tens of thousands of distinct occupations. If we were to think of actual jobs in particular industries and firms, rather than occupations, the number of distinctly different jobs that exist in any large urban labor market is very much greater than even the staggeringly large number of occupations contained in the DOT.

Another characteristic of job markets is that transactions in them represent quite large commitments from the point of view of both sides of the job market transaction. From the employer's side, thousands of dollars of search and of training expenses are often involved, as well as the costs and difficulties of terminating the employment of an unsatisfactory individual if he has the protection of a union, or, as in the case of academic and civil service employment, permanent or even limited tenure. Similarly the new employee, if his decision to accept employment is based on faulty information or is poorly made, may be subject to very heavy costs that may result from a poor decision, loss of income that he might have earned if he had secured better-paying employment, job search costs if he is induced, voluntarily or involuntarily, to enter the job market sooner than he otherwise would have in order to secure more desirable employment. The number of things that can "go wrong" with what initially seemed to be a desirable job or a desirable new employee are legion, and the likelihood of these pitfalls occurring is extremely difficult to predict in advance.

Several years ago, Albert Rees noted that a number of students have criticized labor markets for being inefficient, irrational, and disorderly, proposing that labor exchanges be created to improve their operation.[1] Rees, examining the labor market model underlying this criticism and the proposal for remedy, pointed out that most of these critics assume that local labor markets are analogous to commodity exchanges.

To Rees, the analogy between job markets and commodity exchanges is based on a fundamentally misconceived model of job markets, particularly on a mistaken notion of what kinds of information are required for transactions to take place in the job market. Rather than resembling commodity exchanges, job markets, and the information generated in them, are much closer to used-car markets in character and operation. And, instead of being irrational, inefficient, and disorganized, the local job market, considering the nature of the transactions, generally functions in a reasonably orderly and rational way.

In place of the extensive information appropriate to commodity exchanges, both the job seeker and the potential employer want intensive information. As Rees puts it, the problem facing the employer and job seeker "is not to get in touch with the largest number of potential applicants [potential employers]; rather it is to find a few applicants [potential employers] promising enough to be worth the investment of thorough investigation."[2]

In other words, the job market is from this point of view a screening device that narrows the search process rapidly. But, like David Ricardo's margin of cultivaton, the job search also has extensive and intensive margins. Both the job seeker and the employer looking for a likely worker have the option of searching widely or deeply or pursuing some combination of the two. Search strategy is optimal when the gains to be secured from widening the search equal those gained from deepening it.

Job market information can be inadequate in either the intensive and extensive dimension or both, and one of the goals of a job market information system should be the avoidance of such imbalances. It seems to be inherently easier for governmental agencies to provide information in the extensive dimension than in the intensive. Government information programs may actually, by increasing the imbalance between these two dimensions of job market information, lead the individual job seeker or employer to use more extensive information than he ought to. And, by causing him to take longer to conclude the search, they may have the unintended result of increasing, rather than decreasing, unemployment!

On the other hand, the result may be simply the rejection of the information at hand. Employers and job seekers who perceive that what they really need is more and better intensive information are hardly likely to be led on a wild goose chase, or if they are so led, they are hardly likely to repeat the unhappy experience more than once or twice.

The model, then, that we have of local job markets is in its basic characteristics similar to that proposed by Rees. One of the informational implications of this model is the emphasis it puts on intensive information. Another implication is that, given the economic importance of the typical transaction involved in the job market, both sides of the job transaction must try to acquire information that they can *trust*.

Both the intensive character of job market information and the importance of its being trustworthy lead to several important consequences, particularly when the job market transaction concerns what would be called a "good" job — i.e., relatively well-paid, stable, and part of a job ladder that leads to an even better job. Intensive information does not mean that a *large* amount of information must be transmitted, but rather that particular types of information, varying widely among different individuals and therefore not easily codified and reduced to routine formulas, are the desiderata.

Personal contacts and conversation in an informal context, as many investigations have confirmed, are in many cases likely to produce the kind of information that is trustworthy and relevant to the particular case. It is not surprising, therefore, that "friends and relations" loom so large as a source of data. And it seems likely that the more desirable the job is, the more important the role such informal and personal informational links play.

At the outset, we have emphasized the importance of informal labor market information because of its influence on labor market structure. As Thomas Schelling has observed, "if job vacancies are filled by word of mouth or apartments go to people who have acquaintances in the buildings, and if boys can marry only girls who speak their language, a biased communication system will preserve and enhance the prevailing homogeneities."[3]

In the work history of an individual, certain transition periods are strategic. Every individual, for example, goes through a period of initiation in the world of work and a period of disengagement from work. There is a period of exploration at the beginning of an individual's working life, marked by relatively loose attachment to any particular job. This period is in the usual case a complex mixture of educational and job experience. The exploration of the world of work that takes place is paralleled by an experimentation with different life-styles and exploration of various geographical locations. It is a period of growing awareness of self, increased knowledge about the world of work and the options it offers, and finally of increasingly long-term commitments to places and other people.

This period of exploration, for a large portion of the labor force, gradually or abruptly leads to increasingly stable jobs and the emergence of definite career structures. Light is being thrown on many of these critical transition points by the longitudinal surveys being carried out by Herbert Parnes.[4] The period of transition from exploration to more and more stable work experience has been described, for several types of industries and firms in an urban context, by Marcia Freedman.[5] For the typical white male married worker, the next important transition period may be the process that marks the close of his full-time work experience. But, for many individuals, even in this favored group, several crises may intervene between the exploratory and the disengagement periods. Personal goals may change, and a transition period, described by Dale Hiestand,[6] may occur. Even if personal career goals do not change, an individual may find himself forced by circumstances over which he has no control to change his occupation, his industry attachment, or his geographical location. Such transitions can be abrupt and radical or gradual and involving relatively small changes in occupation or industry attachments.

For women, the patterns of transition are typically quite different. Two transition periods are imposed on the pattern of female white married workers. The first is the withdrawal from the labor force that may accompany child-bearing. This usually comes at about the age that the male worker is concluding the transition from exploration of to establishment in the world of work. Some years later, a woman who has withdrawn from the labor force to have children may reenter the labor force. However, this period of reentrance is marked by numerous constraints, some well known, others requiring further analysis and recognition.

Other transition periods (and transition points) can be distinguished. Older workers face a process of disengagement, either abrupt in the case of compulsory retirement, or long drawn out, during which illness or unemployment lead to a gradual breakdown of attachment to the labor force. Workers attached to particular occupations and industries (police, schoolteachers) go through stages of attachment and disengagement that may come at quite unusual times of life.

Detailed and specific information about the transition periods of particular demographic, occupational, and industrial groups of the labor market should be widely understood and used by labor market specialists. It is during these transition periods that general labor market information is most valuable and frequently most difficult to obtain. Moreover, the kinds of information that are required if an individual is to negotiate these transitions with a maximum of benefit or a minimum of damage are different from the information that is appropriate when an individual is faced with a short period of unemployment or is thinking of changing from one employer to another within the same occupational-industrial context.

## GENERAL AND SPECIFIC JOB MARKET INFORMATION

The work of Gary Becker has made the distinction between general and specific training central to any discussion of the economic consequences of training investments.[7] We can make a similar distinction between the concepts of specific and general job market information. From Becker's point of view the distinction between specific and general training is important in part because the costs and benefits of the two kinds of training are borne or shared in different ways. Our major interest in the distinction between general and specific job market information is not so much concerned with these aspects, important though they are, but rather with the fact that, as we have just stated, general job market information tends to be most valuable at critical transition points in an individual's work history.

Youths, exploring the world of work in search of long-term commitments and careers, need much more than information about which specific local employers are hiring young people. Women reentering the labor force after many years of child-rearing need to know what has happened to the employment prospects of women during the period of their withdrawal from the labor force. Older workers, facing retirement and the prospect of decreasing income along with decreasing physical vigor, need to know how to integrate public and private pensions, increased leisure and opportunities to add to their income through work, often in areas and in occupations that are far removed from those that marked their earlier work life. In sum, general job market information is always of value, but particularly when an individual is contemplating major changes in his relation to the world of work.

### Specific Labor Market Information

Specific labor market information is basically of two sorts. First of all it consists of specific information about the local job market, which enables a worker to find better employment opportunities in his usual line of work. He may act on such information while he is employed, and he particularly needs this kind of information when he is laid off. In general an unemployed worker begins his search by looking for employment that is similar to his last employment experience. Information about the firms that customarily hire workers with his qualifications or about the private and public employment agencies that service such firms is of critical importance. The more specific the information he receives the better. Every study of employment agencies emphasizes the critical importance of specific, accurate, and timely information. It is just because friends and relatives are apt to have such information that they are such an important source of the leads that result in improved jobs or reemployment. The same thing can be said of private employment agencies that specialize in serving a narrow band of occupations and employers.

Another quite different and often overlooked type of specific labor market information is that which an employee possesses about the *internal labor market* of a large employer. This information is analogous to Becker's specific training in that it is of value only so long as an employee remains with a firm. It consists of knowledge about a complex web of personal relationships and institutional rules that make it possible for an individual to negotiate the elaborate maze of interlinked job ladders, upward, downward, and sideways, in response to changes in a firm's output levels and production processes. A moment's reflection on the part of any individual who is employed by a large bureaucratically organized institution about the kinds of labor market information that are of value to him will usually lead to a realization that

53

information about the internal labor market is what he searches for and what he accumulates over time. Because the labor force of a large firm and the rules governing the operation of its internal labor market are together unique to the firm, because so much of internal labor market information circulates through a web of personal relationships, it is inevitable that such information has little value to an individual once he has left a firm. Like specific training, specific internal labor market information undoubtedly reduces the mobility of some employees.

## THE JOB MARKET AS A SORTING AND SCREENING DEVICE: THE ROLE OF QUEUES

The traditional view of the job market emphasizes its competitive character and considers it to be a very complex but more or less automatic sorting device. The image is of an immense number of individuals scurrying around, eagerly seeking out better jobs, incessantly moving through the labor market, guided primarily by wage rates.

One important model of the sorting process in the competitive market relevant to our analysis of the problem of information flows is based on the concept of a queue.[8] At any moment of time there is assumed to be a group of individuals ready to offer themselves for jobs that become available. Generally speaking the position of an individual in a queue is considered to be determined for the most part by the relative productivities of the individuals composing the queue, but it is easy to add to this ranking procedure whatever taste for or discrimination against individuals or groups an employer may have.

However, it is often the case that the group of workers who compose the queue has itself determined on some ranking procedure, not corresponding to the employer's ranking. When the group possesses enough self-descipline and can keep outsiders from crashing the queue (as is the case with unions), it can force an employer to accept to some extent its own ranking rather than his. Finally, the queue is often restricted to a subset of the entire labor force, again by rules that it has set up and enforced.

A number of rules are used, the simplest and one of the most common being that which bases an individual's place in the queue on the moment of his arrival at the queuing point (seniority rules). Union hiring halls generally have adopted some variant of this rule in determining the ranking of union members. It should also be noted that the queuing concept applies to internal as well as external labor markets.

There is nothing in the queue theory of the operation of labor markets to preclude an individual's being in more than one queue at a time, but it is fair to conclude that the queue theory does emphasize an individual's attachment, either to a firm, an industry, or an occupation.

It is worthwhile examining in greater detail the usual queuing situation that faces an employer. His major problem is to estimate the relative productivities of the individuals who make up the queue. How can he best make such estimates, particularly if the composition of the queue is changing over time? One solution to the problem is for the employer to assume that productivities are more or less randomly distributed through the group and that it is costly (or impossible) to determine these in advance of hiring. He can therefore be expected to hire individuals more or less in their chronological order of appearance in the queue and to use their actual performance on the job as a testing period. In this case he will be quite loath to make any long-term commitment at the moment of hiring. But he will use this method of selection only if the actual process of production does enable him to determine fairly quickly the productivity of workers through on-the-job performance.

Since this method of selection and commitment to long-term hiring has marked costs to the employer, he tries to reduce such costs by screening methods designed to eliminate those individuals whose productivity is probably low. Some of what is usually called "discrimination" in the labor market is explainable, even if not justifiable, on this ground. This is because the screening devices that an employer prefers must be easily administered, relatively cheap, and more or less automatic in their incidence. Age, education, honorable discharge from the military service, marital status, nationality, and race, all of them characteristics that are usually easily determined, easily coded in brief data entries, and more or less impersonal, although often highly discriminatory in their operation, become the most common screening devices. They are also easy to file, sort, and build data banks around.

A great deal of what the employer considers to be valuable job market information gets incorporated in these screening devices. To him they sum up the probabilities of success in performance on the job. As he sees them, they represent the experience of many employers including himself over many years. He is often as aware as those who criticize the use of these screening devices that they work injustices in individual cases, but in this sort of hiring situation he usually will not allow himself to be concerned about individual cases. He is looking for a hiring procedure that will produce, over a period of time, a labor force in his firm that has the highest net productivity. If he is more or less satisfied with the quality of his labor force, he will come to believe that the screening devices have been verified by the most important test he can subject them to: They have worked in his own case.

Not only do such screening devices constitute a basic part of the job market information that the employer possesses, but they also become part of the information used by workers and intermediaries in the job market. The effect of these screening devices over time is to make queues for any particular firm, industry, or occupation that are *nonrandom* selections from the total labor force. It is important to keep in mind that the screening devices need not have any direct relationship to individual productivity and that their purpose is to increase the probability that a given group of candidates will on the average have a higher productivity than a group composed of individuals excluded by the screen. It is precisely because the screening devices do not have to be subjected to tests of *direct* and *specific* relevance to productivity that they are so difficult to attack. Indeed it seems likely that if any one screening device is abandoned (or made illegal), another, having much the same content even if it is much altered in appearance, will soon take its place. In sum, queues and the various associated screening devices that get built into them, whether the product of employer or employee action, contain a great deal of the information that is relevant to the operation of the local job market. Such screening devices form an integral part of the general sorting apparatus that in the short run and over long periods mediates between the supply of labor and the demand for it. More important, perhaps, for certain industries and occupations, admission to the queue through the various screens that are associated with it and progression up the queue is the most important determinant of one's life chances in the local job market.

## THE STRUCTURE OF THE LABOR MARKET

The concept of a "dual labor market" has received much attention in the past few years, particularly in the work of such labor market specialists as Michael Piore, Peter Doeringer, and Marcia Freedman. Their work has emphasized the importance of the demographic and sociological features of the labor market. The dual labor market, in their view, consists of (1) the primary labor market, highly structured with high wages, security of employment, the kind of status primarily associated with large-scale oligopolistic firms, and (2) the secondary labor market, relatively unstructured and characterized by low wages, high rates of unemployment, intermittent work, frequent spells of unemployment, part-time work, and dead-end jobs. These secondary labor markets are a feature of a limited group of industries and occupations, primarily small-scale and competitive in character.

These observers also emphasize that it is only movement from the unstructured to the structured labor markets that really offers much opportunity for substantial improvement in the economic and social status of the groups who are now employed within the unstructured labor markets. A recent calculation by Rhona Pavis, for example, indicates that income differentials between blacks and whites are overwhelmingly a matter of occupational distribution. If the employment rate of blacks were to become equal to that of white, leaving blacks in their present occupations and at their present wage levels, it would increase black income by $1.5 billion; if blacks had the same occupational distribution (and wage levels) as white, it would raise black incomes by $14 billion.[9]

The concept of the "dual labor market," then, raises very sharply the issue of the "quality" of jobs and indeed one of the major deficiencies of labor market information as it is now collected and disseminated is that it provides ambiguous and inadequate information about quality. From this discussion it should be clear that the term "quality" of jobs as customarily used contains in fact both qualitative and quantitative components such as relative wage rates, hours of work, and fringe benefits, usually measurable. The more strictly qualitative components are far more complex, involve far greater difficulties of specification, and can only sometimes be subjected to ordinal ranking. Job quality is therefore just the kind of concept that is bound to trouble statisticians, particularly those most strongly in agreement with the recommendations of the Gordon report that each concept should correspond to objectively measurable phenomena and should depend as little as possible on personal opinion and subjective attitudes.

We know all too little about how people learn about the many elements that make up the quality of various kinds of employment and how they assess the information they secure, and we know even less about how to collect, analyze, and disseminate much of this information in any systematic manner. In particular, information dealing with job quality that flows between the structured and unstructured side of the labor markets is probably among the least timely and accurate of all labor market information.

It is not only that there is a lack of information. That would be bad enough. The difficulty is compounded by the fact that much of what is considered to be information that individuals and organizations located on either side possess about the other is erroneous, biased, and distorted, and yet it is such misinformation, much of which centers on the interrelated questions of job quality and human quality, that is peculiarly difficult to erase. Much of it is "in the air" and is not affected at all by direct and supposedly scientific quantitative refutation. A few, dry, even if conclusive, figures do little to alter structures so deeply embedded in one's conception of himself and his world.

Much that determines one's assessment of the qualities of different employment experiences is related to fundamental personal values; these are at the frontiers of labor market information as we now conceive it. But they seem likely to become more and more important in determining how individuals and groups will act, and policy-makers can little afford to be ignorant about such issues.

A number of questions about the nature of employment within the "structured" part of the labor market compared to the "unstructured" part can be answered only by longitudinal studies of great complexity, delicacy, and subtlety. The longitudinal studies conducted by Parnes and others focus on particular demographic groups rather than on the interaction between individual and organization, which would be the focal point of investigations of the "structured" labor markets.

## PORTS OF ENTRY AND THE DUAL LABOR MARKET

Clark Kerr's conception of the labor market as Balkanized calls attention to the crucial role that frontier stations play, the "ports of entry" of his model. Since more desirable employment experiences tend to be located more frequently within the "structured" part of the labor market and since access to this area is at least in part a result of the possession of information about the proper route to follow, such information has value and can in theory be capitalized. Much of what is called "return to human capital" may in fact represent the value of such information.

But it is a curious type of labor market information. As a commentator at a conference of labor market information system researchers held November 1970 in Washington remarked, "Perhaps we would do better to tell a black youth from the ghetto how to get into the carpenters' union than to train him to be a carpenter." Labor market information, in this context and particularly from the point of view of the individual, has greatest value when it tells an individual how to negotiate the obstacle course. But note also that the remark implies that it will in fact make a difference to the youth to be told how one gets into the union. If the information, however, amounts to saying that admission is denied to such a youth, the information is of value only to those who are in a position to change admission procedures.

It is just at this point that one of the most sticky issues of labor market information arises. Breaking down such admission procedures renders information about them, previously of great value to those who possess it, now considerably less valuable. Those who possess such information — privileged information we should call it — can be expected to resist the expropriation of the value of their information.

Probably for the biggest portion of individuals whose jobs are in the "structured" part of the labor market, the institutions that give the basic framework of structure are the large corporations and unions. The structure itself arises out of the interaction of these two institutions. One of the most prominent characteristics of labor market structure in this case is the existence of an "internal labor market," the links between the general labor market and this "internal" market taking the form of recognized "ports of entry" and "ports of exit." Once beyond the "ports of entry," promotion from within is the recognized method of filling vacancies, a method to be bypassed only under accepted rules. When it is necessary for the organization to shrink its labor force, a similar process of demotion, taking the form of "bumping," ensures that employees with seniority will keep their employment as long as possible. Those individuals who are laid off form a pool of potential employees who will be recalled when the organization resumes its usual scale of operations. On the fringes of the organization are individuals who will, or hope to, find a port of entry open to them at some time in the near future.

For a large proportion of American workers, the labor market they confront on a day-to-day basis is the internal labor market of firms about which comparatively less is usually known than about such an unstructured labor market as that of California grape pickers. The customs, operating rules, contractual relationships, and informal characteristics of these internal labor markets differ markedly between industries and, within industries, between establishments. The lifetime earning profiles of individuals, the efficiency with which labor is allocated, and the equity of this allocation are almost certainly influenced to a greater extent by internal labor market arrangements than by any other single element in the institutional make-up of the economy. It is probable that, within the broad framework of American legal conceptions, governmental action in this area, even if it were well-informed about the specific features of internal labor markets, would be relatively constrained. There is a long history of opposition by employers and by organized labor to explicit intervention in the operations of internal labor markets, and federal, state, and local governments have therefore moved quite gingerly in this area.*

_____

*Affirmative action programs represent a move in this direction.

It is also probable that much of the most valuable information about internal labor markets is inherently very difficult to uncover by means of the techniques upon which government has customarily relied for information about the labor market. Because much of it is qualitative, informal, customary in character, usually it is not accessible to outsiders. Although there may be written documents that purport to describe the operation of an internal labor market, for example a union contract or a statement of policy by a company, the exact relationship between such literary and legal documents and the reality of the internal labor market is often difficult to assess.

## STOCKS AND FLOWS

In an understandable effort to get meaningful operational information to assist in the development of appropriate national policy and programs to deal with unemployment in the 1930s, social scientists and statisticians created a system of labor force concepts that has provided the structure for a sophisticated, complex, and expensive statistical program, now embodied primarily in the Current Population Survey (CPS). It is instructive to keep in mind what the conceptual framework created at that time has done to shape our view of the nature of job markets and the world of work.

First, it has tended to downplay the importance of subjective states. Secondly, it has emphasized the importance of three basic stocks — the employed, the unemployed, and a residual stock composed of all others — rather than flows through job markets. Third, it has masked the true heterogeneity of the groups it has created by lumping together activities of very great difference in intensity and in kind and ignoring other activities that might possibly have been included.

For more than a generation we have become accustomed to view the unemployment rate that was derived from the labor force concepts created during the 1930s as the most important diagnostic signal about the efficiency of the operation of the job markets of the country. It is not always clearly understood that the rate of unemployment is a statistical construct of relatively short history, that what it measures is by no means always clear cut, that it may not in fact be the most important barometer of efficiency or well-being, particularly over time, and that it overemphasizes stocks rather than flows through the job market.

The stock of individuals seeking new employment in the job market at any one point in time is the resultant of a complex set of inflows and outflows. Moreover, these flows through the job market are very large. Charles Holt puts the matter succinctly:

> The continual flow of workers, particularly young and unskilled ones . . . annually averages between one third and one half of the total labor force. This annual flow is very large compared to the stock of unemployed workers at any one time . . . . This high flow through the market keeps it in a constant state of flux and makes it respond quickly to changes in economic conditions.[10]

Individuals, particularly the young and all those others who have not secured stable jobs in what we have called the primary labor market, go through the process of job search and job attainment relatively frequently. For them local job market information is at a premium. If the provision of better local job market information to individuals composing these groups were to improve on average the quality of the job that an individual obtains every time he goes through a process of search, the rapid turnover of these groups would improve their relative standing. Important equity effects would result for the young, women, and other minorities.

## JOB SEARCH-TURNOVER THEORY OF UNEMPLOYMENT: THE PHILLIPS CURVE AND JOB MATCHING

The chance that any job seeker will be hired over any period of time is determined by (1) the number of interviews he secures and (2) the probability that an interview will lead to a successful placement. If the time spent looking for an interview is shortened, their number over any given period can be increased. Here, then, is potentially a strategic point of intervention for the provision of detailed and accurate local job market information to the job seeker with the expected effect of decreasing the *number* of unemployed.

Moreover such information can also improve the average "quality" of interviews, increasing the probability that any given interview would lead to a successful placement. This would tend to decrease the average *duration* of unemployment spells. Still another desirable effect of better local job market information should be the increase in the satisfaction of both job seekers and employers, decreasing the flow of workers through the job market by increasing the average duration of employment spells. These arguments add up to a strong claim that one of the effects of improved local job market information will be to shift the Phillips curve somewhat to the left, thereby decreasing the upward pressure on wage rates coincident with a given rate of unemployment.

A major objective of computerized job banks and job matching has been to bring about this kind of shift in the Phillips curve. The high cost of nationwide job banks and job-matching programs demands a careful evaluation of pilot job bank programs. The evaluators of such programs, however, should realize that valid measurement of their cumulative effects cannot in all probability be obtained in the first few years of their operation. This is particularly the case since these programs start with the initial handicap that the employment service has never been able to gain more than a limited penetration of local job markets and, further, that this penetration has unfortunately tended to be higher among industries and occupations characterized by low wages and unstable employment.

Indeed one of the important effects of computerized job banks and job-matching installations should be to increase the penetration rate of the employment service by offering better service to job seekers and employers alike. Moreover there is now a greater willingness to use powerful incentives to get employers to list desirable jobs with the service. Since, as we have just pointed out, the stakes are so high, it is all the more important that those in charge of developing the computerized job bank and job-matching programs have a most sophisticated understanding of the operation of job markets and particularly of the kind of information that job seekers and employers have relied on in the past and the kind that may be appropriate in the future.

## SUMMARY

The general characteristics and operations of the job market, considered as the central "box" in the diagrams of Chapter 2, have been the focus of this chapter. Rather than considering job markets to be analogous to commodity exchanges, our conception of their fundamental character is close to the view of Albert Rees, which emphasizes the uniqueness of many job market transactions and their importance to both employee and employer, both of which characteristics make such job market transactions analogous to transactions in the used car market. Because of these characteristics of job market transactions, intensive and idiosyncratic information is often the desiderata. Such information is therefore often best transmitted informally and through personal relationships. A problem, common to both job seekers and employers, is to narrow their search so that it is possible for them to accumulate the intensive information they need for decisions about job market transactions. A number of screening devices exist that have the effect of narrowing search procedures.

Another way of conceiving the operation of job markets is to consider that they often are similar to a kind of shape-up or queue. If one looks at a job market as composed essentially of a number of job seekers standing in some sort of line, hired only if they are at the head of the line, the most important element of structure then becomes what determines the position of an individual in the queue. Another element that is of central importance is whether queues are composed primarily of particular demographic groups. One view of queuing in job markets asserts that to some considerable extent women, blacks, Chicanos, Puerto Ricans, and other minority groups all too often tend to find themselves confined to a set of queues that provide them with an inferior set of jobs.

The concept of the "dual labor market" can be presented in such terms. The informational implications of the above conceptions of the operation of job markets are important. In particular, serious questions are raised: Can informational inputs directed at job seekers and employers do much to alter the character of job market transactions? Can information, by itself, do much to alter the structure of job markets or to change the place that any individual job seeker occupies in such structures? Another question asks what kind of information is appropriate to job market transactions. Our view of the fundamental character of much of the job markets, particularly in the sectors of the economy that offer stable, well-paid jobs with good prospects for career progress, emphasizes the importance of intensive and informal rather than extensive and formal information. How such information can best be transmitted, and how to give it to individuals who presently find themselves without

61

access to it, is a matter that deserves careful attention and study. The answers to such difficult and important questions should not be expected to be easily obtained. They will most likely come most readily from the joint efforts of many people in many disciplines.

# 5

## THE EMPLOYER PROBE:
## EMPLOYER UTILIZATION
## OF LABOR MARKET
## INFORMATION

As part of our study of labor market information systems, an employer probe was conducted for purposes of obtaining some initial insights into the uses of and need for labor market information among several large* firms located in New York City. Firms providing data in this survey included two book publishing companies, one aircraft parts manufacturing company, one insurance company, a bank, two department stores, two utility companies, one airline, one newspaper, one magazine publisher, an electronics and appliance manufacturing firm, and an aluminum company. Respondents in these firms were encouraged to discuss the major problems faced by their organizations with respect to obtaining, applying, and interpreting labor market information. Particular attention was given to the role of the federal government as a supplier of information. Unstructured interviews, typically conducted with members of manpower planning or personnel departments, served as the main data gathering technique in this study; our findings were supplemented by the results of other published research.**

---

*Each of the firms contacted in this study employed more than 25,000 persons. In addition to labor force size, consideration was given to industrial and occupational diversity in the selection of survey firms.

**As conducted, the employer probe is in no way a "representative" survey of employer practices regarding the utilization of labor market information. Such representativeness would have required a more systematic research effort, with all of the criteria (in addition to those specified in the preceding footnote) relevant to the selection of a sample of firms made conceptually and operationally explicit. This was neither consistent with the purposes of the Labor Market Information Systems study nor possible given the level of resources available for this investigation. Hence the term "employer probe" appropriately describes the nature and intent of our effort—a probe rather than a systematic survey of employer utilization of and need for labor market information.

## INFORMATION UTILIZATION: THE EXTERNAL MARKET

Generally speaking, the acquisition of labor market information stems from the firm's desire to fill job vacancies (whether such vacancies occur because of increases in the demand for labor or the turnover and transfer of personnel). To accomplish this task, the firm must identify sources of supply (as well as changes in and capabilities of the supply) and establish a set of wage rates for the various positions in its occupational structure. In terms of activities related to the external labor market,* then, two important pieces of information that must be obtained are *wage rates and sources of supply.* **

### Wage Rates

With respect to wage rates, the firms in this survey reported making relatively little use of government data. A variety of explanations were offered for this phenomenon, including the following:

(1) Information is not sufficiently disaggregated to be applicable to specific occupations.

(2) Government wage data are not published by industry, so that the firms must turn to alternative sources of supply.

(3) The data include firms and employers of all sizes, whereas the large firms compete among themselves and pay higher wages than (i.e., constitute a different labor market from) smaller firms.

(4) Data are not sufficiently available for high-level professional as well as managerial and executive positions.

(5) Some of the information seems outdated, especially during periods characterized by rapidly rising wages (and prices).

As a result of these perceived shortcomings, the firms turn to sources other than the federal government for wage information. These include employers' associations, trade organizations, personnel associations, and consulting firms.[2] The industry-wide employer association seems to be the most often used source of wage data.

In terms of the specific types of wage information required, the firms placed heavy emphasis on cost-of-living data, primarily for the purpose of determining wage changes. This is apparently done in order to "meet the competition" and to satisfy employee expectations (an "equity" concept).

---

*The discussion in this chapter differentiates between information utilization in the external and internal labor market. The former is the type of market outlined in standard economic theory, where allocation and pricing decisions are determined by (aggregate) economic forces. The latter refers to "an administrative unit such as a manufacturing plant, within which the pricing and allocation of labor is governed by a set of administrative rules and procedures."[1] The uses of and requirements for information by employers differ between these two labor markets.

**This dichotomy is made with reference to labor market information. For example, employers may obtain information about wage rates from one source and information about labor availability from another source. In terms of labor market dynamics, of course, the level and sources of supply are dependent on wage rates.

However, the firms suggest that cost-of-living data are especially crucial to employee transfer policies. For example, in bringing a high-level professional or especially an executive to New York City from another location, the firm must generally establish a new rate of compensation. Respondents in several of the surveyed firms suggested that this is an extremely difficult task, hindered by the lack of good cost-of-living data (the regularly published Consumer Price Index is seemingly not sufficient for this purpose). Therefore, firms frequently turn to consulting organizations to make salary determinations for individual positions or, more commonly, for a study of the entire compensation structure.* Thus the employers contacted in this survey apparently do not solicit or obtain much in the way of wage information from the federal government.

In stating this conclusion, however, we might speculate about the extent to which firms are identifying and emphasizing their information needs rather than their use of existing information. In other words, when asked about the use of government-supplied wage data, employers may focus on their special problem area (e.g., transfer and wage policy for executives), where labor market information and sources of information are difficult to obtain; they overlook their wage-setting activities, where government-provided data are routinely available and used. Without wishing to review the controversy over the use of survey research methods on the one hand and participant observation on the other, we believe it is conceivable that reported practices relative to the utilization of labor market information do not fully reflect the actual uses of such information. If so, our conclusions regarding the firms' use of government-provided wage data should be modified accordingly.

### Sources of Supply

Here too our responses indicate that large firms in New York City do not view government as an important source of labor market information (or, more specifically in this case, as a source of labor supply). Vacancies are not filled by drawing upon the resources of government. A variety of explanations were offered in support of this behavior. Perhaps the most often cited is the notion that the Employment Service provides a low-quality worker, one who is unreliable and not as productive as employees obtained from other sources. Respondents in the surveyed firms also suggested that people referred by the Employment Service are interested primarily in retaining their unemployment benefits (and thus must appear to be looking for work) and not in securing jobs. In the same vein, it is argued that "good workers" or "high-quality

---

*Eight of the firms contacted during the employer probe reported that, within the last year, they had contracted with consulting firms to study various aspects of wage policy. Five of these efforts involved executive compensation, with three devoted specifically to intra-company transfer policy.

employees" avoid the "unemployment office"; they look for jobs on their own.*

Whether or not these observations reflect processes of selective perception or more objective "facts," it does appear that, with the exception of some low-skilled occupations, large employers in New York City generally refrain from using the federal-state Employment Service as a source of labor supply. One of the policy implications that emerges from this finding is that the unemployment and employment functions of the Employment Service should be clearly separated (in terms of operations, staffs, and even geography).** This is neither an original nor a recent proposal,[3] but one that is further supported by the findings of the employer probe.

Among the sources of supply and/or recruitment methods used by the surveyed firms were the following: private employment agencies; advertising in newspapers and trade journals, on television and radio; labor organizations and union hiring halls; college and university recruiting; referrals from presently employed workers; and referrals from personnel offices of other firms (usually in the same industry).

The extent and usage of these varies considerably by occupation and the general level of economic activity. Private employment agencies, as expected, are used primarily for high-level professional, technical, and executive personnel (although some firms maintain a strict policy of promotion from within for executive and managerial jobs). Unions serve as a source of supply for highly skilled craft tradesmen, a relatively small proportion of all workers in the surveyed firms. Direct hiring at the gate commonly occurs in semiskilled and unskilled laboring positions. College recruiting is used for a wide variety of white-collar and professional occupations, especially to fill vacancies in entry-level positions. Advertising in the various media is used largely, but not exclusively, for technical and professional jobs, including those that are quite specialized in nature. These formal recruitment patterns are similar to those evidenced by employers in other large urban labor markets.[4]

Another recruitment technique used by New York City employers included in this probe is the solicitation of referrals from currently employed workers. Some of the firms used this method to locate executives amd managers, others to attract professional personnel. More commonly, however, the firm's existing labor forces served as a source of supply for clerical, sales, and other assorted white-collar workers. Typical of these practices was that of a major book publisher who paid his clerical employees $50 for each referral that

---

*At the same time, however, employers support the policy of requiring a person to look for work in order to retain unemployment insurance benefits. Thus firms encourage individual search behavior in the labor market, while complaining about the quality of these "searches." Perhaps judgments about worker capabilities reflect an element of self-fulfilling prophecy rather than actual measures of quality (and quality differences).

** It may be argued, however, that unemployment insurance recipients, having had at least reasonably continuous employment experience in the past, have an advantage over other registrants of the employment service. Separation of the unemployment insurance and employment functions might exacerbate rather than resolve the labor market problems of the latter group.

resulted in a new hire.* A similar practice was evidenced by a large department store, which paid substantial bonuses to buyers who suggested potential employees. Almost four-fifths of the surveyed companies used this recruitment method (i.e., source of supply), although the extent of usage varied considerably across companies.

Perhaps the primary rationale for use of the informal labor market as a source of supply is the built-in "screening" process that operates here. Respondents in the New York City firms repeatedly stated that "high-quality" personnel were obtained through employee referrals. This was specifically linked to the notion that current employees had knowledge of both job requirements and applicant capability and were thus unlikely to recommend a person who could not perform the job (or, more precisely, perform the job well). Furthermore, since the current employee's personal judgement is involved in this selection process, he is unlikely to refer a person to his own firm who is incapable of performing well on the job.[5] From the firm's viewpoint, then, the informal labor market (currently employed workers) is a valuable and often used source of labor supply, because it yields benefits that outweigh the costs associated with using it.**

This conclusion, however, should be tempered by the realization that recruitment (and screening) through the existing labor forces may prevent some people from obtaining jobs *who are nevertheless capable of performing the job.* Like some other institutionalized personnel practices,[6] this method of employee selection results in informal labor market discrimination. Policies intended to overcome labor market discrimination, if they are to be effective, must deal directly with (and perhaps offer alternatives to) employers' continued use of the employee referral recruitment channel.

With regard to the effects of the level of aggregate economic activity on recruitment practices, respondents in all but two of the surveyed firms noted that the slowdown in the economy that occurred during the latter half of 1969 and the early part of 1970 had caused a reduction in virtually all forms of recruitment, especially college recruiting and direct advertising. Most of the respondents commented that their firms were now faced with a "buyers'" market, a situation that contrasted notably with the tight labor markets of the middle and late 1960s. Put differently, a general loosening of the labor market causes employers to search for personnel less frequently at both the intensive and extensive margins (especially the latter).[7]

Thus, private employers included in this probe apparently want relatively little from the federal government with respect to labor market information. While several respondents mentioned that their firms used a special piece of information (e.g., a wage rate for custodians, the size of the labor force in a New York suburb), none paid particular attention to regularly published

---

*In the year preceding this survey, *all* additions to this firm's clerical labor force were obtained through employee referrals!

**One would like to be more precise about the specific costs and benefits of such labor market activity, but this would require that firms be much more systematic in their data-gathering and recordkeeping activities than they are at present.

unemployment statistics. Some concern was evidenced about the changing composition of the labor force, but, on closer inspection, this seemed to stem primarily from the managerial problems created by the employment of white-collar and especially professional workers in large organizations rather than from an interest in the availability of labor supplies. In any case, virtually no attention was given to (or a need expressed for) government data that elucidate specific changes in the composition of the labor force.* Furthermore, there seems to be little awareness on the part of employers of some of the more recent empirical work in the area of labor market operations. For example, most of the respondents queried were unfamiliar with such concepts as the "reserve labor force"[8] or the "dual labor market."[9] (A distinction was made, however, between primary and secondary workers, mainly to explain wage differentials between male and female employees.) This is somewhat surprising in view of recent governmental activity undertaken to summarize and widely disseminate the resuls of research on labor markets and human resources utilization.[10]

Some respondents indicated that their firms would like to have additional information concerning labor force composition when moving to a new location (although they did not suggest what price they would be willing to pay for these data), but, here too, the information provision capacities of the federal government were downgraded or rejected. In contrast, the firms do have access to (and make use of) this type of labor market information from state and local governments.**

Finally, of all the various types of labor market information discussed in this probe, employers were most concerned with obtaining accurate wage data (including those pertinent to wage levels, wage changes, and cost-of-living indexes). These data, according to private employers, could be most appropriately provided by the federal government.

## INFORMATION UTILIZATION: THE INTERNAL MARKET

When we examine employer utilization of labor market information, attention should not be restricted solely to the external market. Instead, we should move beyond the recruitment and hiring functions to a consideration of the internal labor market and its components: skills inventories, promotion policies and practices, training programs and investments, and selection models and processes.

The use of a skills inventory enables a firm to maintain a systematic record of its in-house human resources. In this (relatively narrow) sense, human

---

*However, Margaret Thal-Larsen of the University of California at Berkeley has told the authors that, in a recent study of employment practices of San Francisco Bay area employers, information regarding "labor demand/supply developments in specific occupations" was second only to current wage rates as the most often required type of data in firms' daily operations.

**Since some of this information at the local level results from federal requirements for state employment service systems, the federal government does play a larger role in the provision of information than employers realize.

capital is treated analogously to physical capital.[11] The increasing use of skills inventories as a tool of manpower planning and administration is due in large measure to advances in computer technology.[12] It would be inaccurate, however, to suggest that maintenance of such inventories is a standard practice among the firms included in this study, for such is clearly not the case. Only four of the firms included in our probe had a formal skills inventory system in operation as of early 1970.*

Additionally, there are major differences in the way in which skills inventories are used by the various New York firms. In some cases, the inventory simply replaces outmoded and less elegant personnel files but continues to serve the same (rather limited) purposes. Bits and pieces of information are recorded amd maintained but rarely retrieved or used in an analytical fashion. In other firms, the skills inventory is used as a "search" device, typically in situations where job vacancies have occured. Here, the employer attempts to determine if he can fill a position from within rather than incurring the costs of recruiting and hiring from the external market. This procedure yields useful labor market information of an internal nature. Respondents in the surveyed firms were clearly dubious about the government's ability to provide assistance in this regard. Indeed, several personnel specialists were quite critical of glamorous "job-matching" schemes (especially those associated with advanced computer applications) that tend to emphasize fitting those looking for work to existing job vacancies but neglect the matching function in internal labor markets.**

With regard to promotion policies and practices, all but one firm emphasized a preference for promotion from within. This policy was especially prevalent in the filling of managerial and executive positions but was also applied to a wide variety of white-collar occupations.† Several of the respondents mentioned that career paths are specifically designated for individuals at the time they are hired into entry-level positions, so that adherence to a policy of promotion from within also governs the firm's recruitment and selection policies.

Whether (and to what extent) a policy of promotion from within derives from employer preferences or relatively loose external labor markets is unclear, but this pattern of progression within the internal labor market reflects the fact

---

*Five other firms, however, were in the process of operationalizing such inventories. Recall, though, that only large employers in New York City were included in the probe; it is unlikely that the extent of usage of skills inventories would be any greater among small and medium-size firms (and it would probably be considerably smaller due to the costs of installing such systems).

**We might well include here those who would look for work if they thought jobs were available. A job-matching system is partially dependent on job vacancy data, and, if these data were widely disseminated as a form of labor market information, presumably some persons previously discouraged by the lack of work opportunities would be attracted back into the labor force.

†Similar findings were obtained in a recent study of employer manpower policies conducted in the San Francisco Bay area.[13] Failure to follow a promotion-from-within policy is typically associated with peculiarities of the industry.

that only a few entry-level jobs (i.e., "ports of entry"[14]) exists within the occupational structure of the firm. Additionally, a policy of promotion from within suggests that a firm may have invested in "specific" rather than "general" training.[15] The value of a specifically trained employee increases only to the firm providing the training, not to any other firm (i.e., the benefits of training are not transferable). This may seem surprising in an age when increased specialization is a pervasive educational philosophy, but the personnel specialists interviewed in this study indicated that, for a considerable period of time after they are initially hired, most employees are simply not too productive. More precisely, they are being paid more than the value of their marginal product. Subsequently, when knowledge (i.e., training) specific or peculiar to the organization has been gained, this situation changes. Investments in training made by the firms apparently cause them to consider the internal labor market as a source of supply before turning to the external market.*

Finally, the various selection processes used by the New York firms contacted in this study were examined in light of their implications for labor market information. Not surprisingly, job "requirements" or "qualifications" were modified downward during periods of tight labor markets and raised when loose markets obtained. These practices were most commonly applied to unskilled and semiskilled positions but also occurred in the recruitment and hiring of some white-collar workers, particularly sales and paraprofessional personnel.

Employed in this fashion, selection processes respond to the availability of labor supplies rather than being based on demonstrable relationships between qualifications and job performance.[16] Information regarding these linkages — i.e., between "predictor" and "criterion" variables** — would seem to be especially valuable in implementing the manpower or human resources management function. As the results of our probe indicate, however, in only two cases did firms attempt to determine systematically the relationship between selection requirements and job performance. In the first instance, a magazine publisher was conducting a validation study of a test battery used in the selection of professional personnel; the second firm, a manufacturer of airplane components, was similarly examining the use of formal schooling level in the selection of operatives. The other firms, including those with operational skills inventory systems, were either unaware of (and, in some cases, uninterested in)

---

*A policy of promotion from within may also contribute to the setting of excess "qualifications" for entry-level jobs. This would occur when new employees are not hired primarily for entry positions but, rather, to be trained for and promoted to higher-level jobs.

**The terminology used here derives from industrial and personnel psychology. Simply stated, the typical selection process rests on the classical validation model which seeks to link predictors (eg., attitudinal, demographic, and socioeconomic characteristics of job applicants) with criteria (measures of "success" or performance). Ideally this process screens out those incapable of performing the job and differentiates ability to perform among those remaining.[17]

this problem or reluctant to modify current practices because of uncertainty about the replacement criteria to be used in selecting a labor force.*

Of course the conventional personnel selection and placement model rests on the assumption that, with respect to the acquisition of manpower, the problem facing the firm is one of choosing (or determining how to choose) from among an excess supply of applicants. The efficacy of this assumption, however, is related to conditions in the external labor market. A loose market will generally yield excess supplies of labor, and selection processes are then directed toward choosing the most "qualified" personnel. Under the pressures of a tight labor market, however, job requirements may be modified downward and, in cases of sustained high levels of demand, virtually abandoned.** Emphasis on the fluidity of so-called selection criteria raises numerous implications for informal labor market discrimination, human resources utilization, and employment problems generally; these selection processes and other components of internal labor markets should be considered of prime importance in the development of both conceptual and operational foundations of a comprehensive labor market information system.

Finally, as in the case of the personnel selection process, the utilization of labor market information seems at least partially related to the general level of economic activity. The results of this probe suggest that employers demand more (i.e., are willing to pay more for) labor market information during periods of economic expansion and growth than during periods of economic decline. When wage rates are being bid up and shortages of labor are evidenced, employers invest more heavily in labor market information – information concerning sources of supply, occupational trends, wage rates, and job qualifications (including their own). Conversely, the loosening of labor markets is associated with a reduction of investments in labor market information. It is perhaps not coincidental that the proliferation of concern with corporate manpower planning and labor market information manifested during the late 1960s occured at a time when the United States was experiencing its tightest labor market conditions since the Korean War.[19] Perhaps the implication of this analysis for government policy-makers is that sustained economic growth is still the primary mechanism for alleviating employment and human resource management problems – and not incidentally for spurring increased utilization of labor market information.

## A Policy Note

In view of the discussion presented above, the federal government may have a role to play in connection with the qualifications-performance nexus.

---

*Disinterestedness or reluctance may no longer suffice with respect to the maintenance of selection devices that unfairly discriminate against individuals. In the recent *Duke Power* case, the U.S. Supreme Court ruled that employment tests (and other "qualifications") must be related to job performance if they are used in selecting from among job applicants.[18]

**In this discussion, we have ignored the impact of changing economic conditions on wage rates. Certainly employers adjust wages in response to changing labor market conditions. Not all of these responses take the form of wage adjustments, however; others include revision of selection standards and extension of the geographic scope of search.

Specifically, a series of pilot studies might be undertaken for purposes of evaluating the validity and reliability of various selection devices. Particular attention would be directed toward determining the extent to which individual characteristics (e.g., attitudinal, demographic, and socio-economic) actually serve as predictors of job performance.

An initial pilot study might focus on the use of tests in the employment process. Aptitude and personality tests are widely used in the internal labor market operations of private (and public) employers, affecting large numbers of people in different occupations.[20] The apparent failure to validate these tests properly and, more importantly, the lack of evidence concerning the use of employment tests in the selection process[21] suggest that this would be an appropriate point to begin investigation of the operation of the internal labor market. Alternatively (or additionally), a pilot study of the use of schooling level as a selection criterion might be undertaken. The objectives would be the same as those that guide a study of personnel testing; to determine the validity and reliability of selection devices with a view toward eliminating those that unfairly discriminate against individuals in the labor market.

The details of the kinds of studies advocated above need not be reviewed here, but they should be designed so as to draw upon a variety of groups in the labor force, especially those excluded (explicitly or otherwise) from specific occupations.

The results of these studies should be widely disseminated; it is hoped they would influence the formulation of employer manpower policies. Beyond this, however, and in view of the reluctance of employers to modify established selection practices — a reluctance often reinforced by institutional constraints — the findings of these studies might serve as the basis for extending or creating federal legislation that seeks to provide an employment process relatively free from the effects of unfair discrimination. This is particularly important during periods of loose markets, when the nefarious effects of selection processes weigh more heavily on some labor force groups than they do during periods of sustained economic growth. Finally, if used in the making of manpower policy at both the aggregate and firm levels, the findings of these studies, which in the terminology of this probe are pieces of labor market information, would improve the operation of both internal and external labor markets.*

---

*The former would be accomplished by giving the employer a larger labor supply, thus (assuming *ceteris paribus* conditions) lowering unit labor costs; the latter, by causing a more efficient allocation of resources in the production and distribution of goods and services. It is one of the anomalies of current selection processes that, while they apparently allow a firm to choose a "qualified" employee, they often screen out persons capable of performing on the job, thus contributing to higher wage rates (and unit labor costs) than would otherwise exist. From this standpoint, then, employers should support the study of current selection devices; they could be no worse off and might be considerably better off because of these studies than they are at present.

# 6

## CAREER
## GUIDANCE

In Chapter 2, we indicated that among the major institutional intermediaries that intervene between the manpower subsystem and the employment subsystem is career guidance. As part of a series of illustrative investigations of institutional facets of the labor market that have important information functions, utilize particular types of labor market information, and disseminate it in ways that have strategic impact on the efficiency and equity of the entire manpower-employment system, our probe of career guidance as it presently exists in the United States is designed to lead to a set of recommendations that recognize the unique potential of guidance while keeping in mind its limitations and its linkages to other labor market institutions.

### DEFINITION AND ROLE OF CAREER GUIDANCE

By career guidance we mean the formal activities of a number of agencies and institutions, some of them located within schools, others in the Employment Service and in organizations like the Veterans Administration and the Department of Defense, and others under the aegis of various profit and nonprofit institutions. Our primary focus, however, will be on guidance within the general framework of the nation's schools and colleges.[1]

We have selected the institution of career guidance as it is found in the nation's schools for special attention in part because we have wished to emphasize throughout this volume our sense of the importance of developmental and dynamic processes that determine the long-run outcome of an individual's experiences in the job market. Career guidance, by its very nature, asserts the proposition that it is possible, through appropriate intervention on the part of professionally trained experts, to alter the process of development of young people in ways that will lead to improved careers.

At the heart of career guidance, as we believe the process should ideally unfold, is a parallel development of awareness of self (personal assessment) and information about the world of work, including knowledge of occupations, but by no means limited to such information. Through the creative application of guidance techniques, the developing individual gradually fuses these two developmental processes so that he is in a position to match objective possibilities in the world of work with his own aptitudes, inclinations, and values. One of the critically important aspects of the process is that the client, for example the maturing adolescent in high school, must be fully involved in the process at all stages.

What have been the major sources of inputs utilized by guidance counselors and how appropriate are they to the kind of fusion we have sketched? On the one hand, personal assessment "has traditionally relied on psychometric methods and findings; career information has relied on occupational publicatons."[2] The student is frequently confronted with test results whose significance he little understands. He often has little opportunity to develop a relationship with a guidance counselor in which he can learn to assess, in his own language and at his own pace, his personal development. On the other hand, he is exposed to diverse experiences that begin to acquaint him with the world of work. Those offered by the guidance counselor frequently take the form of suggestions to read about occupations. The primary sources are the federally sponsored *Occupational Outlook Handbook* and the *Occupational Outlook Quarterly*. Thousands of copies of the *Handbook* and the *Quarterly* are sold to the guidance departments of the nation's schools and colleges. But it is difficult to assess to what extent the guidance counselors themselves really use (or understand the limitations of) this material.

The training of the guidance counselor has tended to treat separately the functions of personal assessment and the provision of career information, although, as Ginzberg emphasizes, they should be "inextricably interwoven."[3] Instead of the fusion of the two developmental processes, the present situation of the guidance counselor within many school systems and the schools themselves has tended to produce a separation of the two processes. What is imparted then comes to seem artificial and lifeless to the student, making his participation in the guidance function perfunctory at best and the source of resentment and irritation at worst. Little wonder that, for many students — particularly for those who need it most, the potential or actual dropout, the student who reads poorly, who does not possess the informational resources of the white middle-class student — guidance is seen as simply one more arm of an authoritarian administration rather than a valuable ally in the search for a meaningful career.

Several important considerations emerge from this cursory review of the "ideal" process of career guidance and the actuality in many of the nation's high schools. The first has to do with the linkages that *should* exist in an ideal information network and the *actual* linkages that may have come about in the day-to-day functioning of institutions. Let us refer again to our model of the total information system that links together the manpower-employment system to identify the important linkages that *should* have developed between the career guidance function and other labor market institutions. An examination of these linkages will illustrate both the importance of a systems view of the labor market and emphasize how in the concrete instance of the guidance function, linkages either do not exist at all or have developed in so truncated a fashion that they make it difficult for the guidance function to attain what might have been expected from it.

Career guidance has a primary link to students but includes many other client groups whose importance may very well increase in the near future. Since the relationship between students and guidance counselors is inevitably strongly influenced by what parents and parent organizations think the role of the guidance counselor in the school should be, one of the most important tasks is to develop linkages between guidance and parent organizations. Moreover, the status of the career guidance counselor and the support he receives from the community at large depends largely on what the community, particularly parents and parent organizations, perceive the function of guidance to be. If the community perceives that guidance can and does improve the chances that their children will be able to make better career choices, it is likely that the guidance function within the schools will receive both financial and other types of support, particularly in the form of close ties with business and commerce. Such support will enable it to resist pressures from schools and school superintendents that may otherwise tend to transform the guidance function into a subordinate and distorted position within the school system. It is to this second relationship of guidance within the manpower system, between the schools and guidance, that we now turn.

Although guidance in the schools of the United States started with a very definite orientation toward the provision of information that would lead to improved occupational choice, it has from the beginning had an ambiguous relationship to the teaching and administrative functions of schools. Educators have properly resisted a tendency, strong in the United States, to consider schools in a purely utilitarian and primarily vocational frame of reference. Although in general accepting the public's view that schools had to prepare young people for useful and productive lives, teachers have asserted that schools have several functions that transcend the importance of such preparation for the world of work. The transmission of essential moral and cultural values and the preparation of a select few for creative intellectual activity have always seemed to important segments of the teaching community to relegate the more mundane provision of occupational skills, even if it took very general forms, to a subordinate position. The public school has often managed to communicate its uneasy relationship to the world of work to the guidance counselor himself. What has been the result? Rather than concentrating his efforts on assisting the 50 percent or more of high school students who could be expected to enter the labor market after graduation, the counselor has often found himself involved heavily in placing students in colleges (and, since parents soon responded to the general impression that was developing that colleges were the key to upward economic and social mobility, they too pushed the guidance counselor in this direction) and guiding adolescents through trouble spots in their personal development.

75

The guidance counselor in general has not been in a postion to push successfully for major changes in school curriculum or in the relation between academic and work experience that transforms the school experience of non-college-bound students into as constructive an introduction as possible to the kinds of work that come closest to meeting their needs. A growing recognition of this problem has led to a division of functions in some of the larger urban high schools, particularly in New York City, in the form of a specially appointed "college-bound" counselor who works exclusively with such students while the other counselors specialize in the career needs of the remaining students.

In the system of labor market information that we have sketched, the guidance counselor should be linked to the school and its administration, not as a staff member providing services on call to the administration and the teaching staff, but rather as a quasi-independent professional able to inform the school about the career imperatives of its students. This would avoid the danger pointed out by Ginzberg: "Professionals can criticize; employees cannot."[4]

## GUIDANCE AND GOVERNMENT

In addition to its links to parents, students, teachers, and school administrators, guidance is linked closely to other governmental institutions. The training of guidance counselors is subsidized to various degrees by a number of federal programs, located in different agencies. Career guidance counselors receive and disseminate information, originating primarily in the Department of Labor, about the characteristics of occupations and their outlook. The focus of these occupational information programs is on the characteristics of occupations and the aptitudes and training appropriate for them. Unfortunately, it is much more difficult for these programs to provide specific labor market information, something that students and guidance counselors both agree is desirable. Nor in general does occupational outlook information convey a large amount of information to young people about the world of work and the ways one negotiates its opportunities and obstacles. In addition many of those students who most need the information tend to find the format and the style of delivery forbidding and not easily utilized. The Department of Labor is of course aware of such problems, and many innovations in the delivery of this information have been made in the recent past.

Another problem, inherent in the nature of the information, is that the *Occupational Outlook Handbook* obviously cannot describe all the occupations listed in the *Dictionary of Occupational Titles*. It has been necessary to select some 700 occupations, and it is very difficult to find a criterion for which occupations should be included that would be acceptable to all client groups. Should it be the 700 occupations most important to the national economy? Should it include those occupations that in sum contribute most to employment? Should it be the expanding occupations? Should it be the occupations that are most likely to offer employment to the client groups that most need occupational guidance, and if so, who are they?

A point that needs emphasis in regard to the linkage between guidance and occupational information agencies of the government is the critical importance of a feedback of information from guidance to the occupational information specialists. As we have emphasized from the outset, career guidance depends for its success on the fusion by the client of knowledge about himself and knowledge of the world of work, leading to improved decision-making. The last stage of the transmission is as important as the initial stages. Only if occupational information specialists have an adequate comprehension of the whole developmental process leading to career decisions can they hope to contribute as efficiently as possible to the process. Thus it is essential that career guidance counselors communicate to the occupational information specialists just how the information that they generate is in fact being used.

## THE SPECIAL ROLE OF USES

Career guidance stands in a double relationship to one agency of the government, the United States Employment Service (USES), a relationship made even more complicated by the fact that the Employment Service is a joint state-federal operation. The Employment Service local offices offer career guidance and counseling under their own wing. Guidance counselors associated with schools, nonprofit institutions, and other community agencies ought to be able to find in the counseling areas of USES a common set of professional policies, practices, and goals. The major informational weakness of school career guidance counselors, both clients and counselors would probably agree, has been a lack of concrete, specific local labor market information. In just this respect, however, the guidance function of USES ought to be very strong, while in the area of personal assessment the reverse might be expected to be the case, because of the difficulty of developing in-depth relationships with clients.

Moreover, the present orientation of USES, the assignment to it of the mission of serving individuals and groups who have been relatively disadvantaged in the job market, should provide the analytical insights and practical operational knowledge about what is involved in bringing such individuals into fuller and more rewarding participation in the labor force.

Career guidance counselors in schools and their counterparts in USES share another concern. Both are involved with client groups who are at critical transition points in their relation to the labor market, clients who are unsure of themselves and who lack knowledge of the opportunities the job market may offer and of the barriers that stand in the way of their realizing these opportunities.

It would seem, therefore, that career guidance has everything to gain by the development of the closest professional and operational ties between the guidance activities of USES and other forms of career guidance. In practice, however, the factors that would seem to provide occasion for the closest cooperation are also responsible for the generally tenuous linkages that exist in fact in a great number of schools between USES and the school guidance personnel.

We have had occasion in other chapters to point out that the Employment Service has been able to service only a fraction of the labor market, from the point of view of both employers and job seekers. We do not need to review the complex set of forces that have historically brought about this situation. A number of high-level reports have pointed out how deeply rooted the situation is, and the work of Margaret Thal-Larsen in San Francisco illustrates vividly the tension and ambiguities in the day-to-day operations of local offices involved in the conscientious attempts of USES to fulfill its complex mission.

The problem can be stated simply. The Employment Service's ability to serve a total range of occupations in the labor market appears to be inversely related to the intensity of its efforts to service the needs of the most disadvantaged members of the labor force. As things stand at the present time, therefore, the Employment Service seems to many school career guidance personnel to offer inadequate access to desirable occupational careers. Although it has labor market information that is specific and knows a great deal about the way the labor market operates, particularly for the most disadvantaged, its knowledge is one-sided, truncated, and limited by and large to the least desirable part of the job market. It is easy enough for anyone to gain access to the secondary labor markets. The problem is to gain access to the primary labor markets, where stable, well-paying jobs with career progression are located. It is useless to talk about improving the linkages between Employment Service and other career guidance counselors until this problem is squarely faced and steps are taken to surmount it. Particularly is this the case for counselors whose primary clients are young people, a good proportion of whom are high school graduates only, frequently black and central-cities residents to boot.

## CAREER GUIDANCE AND THE EMPLOYER-EMPLOYEE COMMUNITY

The guidance profession has been aware for a number of years that it was necessary to develop as far as possible linkages with employers. In addition, it has come to realize that one of the most effective ways of communicating labor market information to its clients, particularly the most distrustful portion, black youth from the central cities, is to use young workers, in particular black youth, who are able to convey their experiences in the language styles of their clients and with a degree of realism, specificity, and believability that the professional career guidance counselor cannot hope to equal.

But there are a number of other facets to the linkages between school guidance personnel and the world of the employer-employee that should be noted. These elements again illustrate the complex and multifaceted character of labor market information. For example, a constant complaint of employers, heard in increasing volume and with an increasing tone of exasperation, is that young people know nothing about the world of work even in the most elementary fashion.

Employers are not asking here for young people who are highly sophisticated and skilled in a profession. The burden of their complaints is that young people do not know what is expected of them in a general sense as employees.

In punctuality, willingness to take orders, compliance with standards of dress and comportment, in these and a host of other dimensions, many young people seem to large numbers of employers to be ill-prepared for the world of work. And employers tend to blame the schools for these lacks. And, where schools offer programs that are vocationally oriented, the business community is often of the opinion that the training is largely on obsolete equipment and lacks realism in terms of the demands of occupations. Indeed many employers prefer to hire totally untrained people rather than trying to cope with what they feel to be badly trained young people who find it difficult to accept the fact that their training is faulty.

Looking at the linkage of guidance to employer-employee from the side of the career guidance counselor in the school, it is worth noting again that one of the chief problems he faces in helping young people develop a career strategy is his lack of specific and down-to-earth information about the world of work. He is apt to lack a feel for the actuality of occupations, to be unable to convey what it is like to be employed in typical occupations. Several possibilities are open to the guidance counselor to remedy this situation. He can incorporate, first in his training and, later on, in his activity as a counselor, direct contact with employers, either as observer or, better yet, as participant-observer. Even though it will be impossible for him to sample more than a small fraction of the possible occupations in any labor market, direct contact with employers cannot but affect his approach to the task of counseling. His perceptions of what workers want to know about the work situation will be keener and he will understand more fully that the transmission of occupational information is only one part of the totality of labor market information that makes it possible for young workers to determine what should be their preferred strategy in exploring the world of work.

Another approach the counselor can and does use is to develop with employers programs that permit students themselves to be exposed to work situations. The value of these work-study programs and similar ones aimed at giving young people work experience that assists them in making improved career choices derives less from the concrete information about specific occupations that the young person secures than from the feel it gives him for the world of work. Work-study programs and career guidance in general would be considered a waste of time in a society in which the school-leaving age is 14 or so, which has an extensive apprenticeship system and in which sons follow their fathers' occupations. In contemporary American society, by contrast, school-leaving ages have steadily increased and the range of occupations, firms and geographical areas that face first entrants into the labor force is generally beyond the comprehension of even the best informed. Youth is supposed to exercise free choice and by this exercise find income and satisfaction. Faced with such conditions, however, it is understandable that the young should feel the problem of choice to be overwhelming.

The business community is of course concerned about the long-run implications of a possibly highly unsatisfactory introduction of the oncoming generation to the world of work. This sense of concern could provide the basis for the creation of more conscious and creative linkages between the profession of career guidance and employers. To the extent that such linkages are related to real problems in local job markets and seem to promise more satisfactory outcomes of individual career choice, the situation of the guidance counselor could be radically changed. Hitherto he has been perhaps too much dependent on the school administrator as a staff member of the school who could be asked to help with a number of school problems that had little to do with his central mission of assisting youth and others to make better career choices. Linked to parents and community, particularly to the business community as well as the school, the career guidance counselor would find it easier to assert his professional identity, while at the same time vastly increasing his sense of both the needs of his primary clients and the possibilities of assistance that he can draw upon from various sectors of the community. Many of the New York City schools offer examples of just such networks of businessmen's advisory councils and realistic work-study programs that provide strong support to the counselor's efforts.

Another set of linkages involves various agencies and individuals that provide support inputs to the career guidance counselor. One group of support personnel is made up of psychologists, psychotherapists, and social workers. As Ginzberg puts it, "If guidance counselors are to develop competence they cannot at one and the same time be informed sources of career information and assistance and continue to serve as psychotherapists or administrators. They must rely more on referrals to psychologists and social workers."[5]

Another kind of support personnel is essential if guidance is to develop satisfactory outreach programs. In every type of information program and training program aimed at demographic and geographical groups that have had severe labor market problems, it is clear that one of the most difficult hurdles that must be surmounted at the outset is bringing the members of the target population into an initial relationship with the program characterized by some minimum degree of hope and trust. Ginzberg has pointed out that,

> as experience with the loosely attached in the labor market has demonstrated, there are critical functions, such as outreach, which can be performed best by support personnel. A white female counselor may guide a youth from the ghetto just as well as a black male counselor, but she is unlikely to be able or willing to go into the ghetto and find him and coax him into the office for service.[6]

## SUMMARY

A well-rounded labor market information program under the aegis of the guidance counselor should include a wide range of direct work experience and indirect exposure to the world of work through various media. The development of work-study programs is but one example of the complex set of linkages that constitute the groundwork, so to speak, of a labor market information system. And such programs illustrate the profound effect very general changes in the structure of labor markets can have on such linkages and related information flows.

Successful career guidance points up the fact that labor market information is much more than knowledge of occupations or of such easily quantifiable matters as wage rates and hours of work. And it also demonstrates that much of this labor market information cannot easily be conveyed by the usual information media — books, magazines, radio, conferences, classes, television, and so forth. Success in guidance seems to depend on an amalgam of information furnished through formal channels and informal on-the-job learning with the guidance counselor serving as coordinator of the two.

# LABOR MARKET INFORMATION
# AND EDUCATION

No discussion of the prerequisites for effective manpower policy, including basic informational needs, can proceed very far without systematic attention being given to the role of education in the processes by which the economy is staffed and the needs and aspirations of citizens are met.

The fact that formal education plays other parts in the nation's life than those bearing on the structure and functioning of the economy and the economic well-being of people need not detain us here; one may simply concede that there are "consumption" as well as "production" benefits associated with education. Even educators, however legitimately and sincerely they may affirm the loftiest of ideals regarding education, would allow for the play of utilitarian values. Indeed, most would argue that the multiple benefits of formal education go hand in hand.

Indeed, in the history of the Republic there has never been much doubt that formal education could serve material ends while simultaneously serving to deepen the understandings and broaden the perspectives of those who attend to labs, classes, and disciplined reading. And, until quite recently, history collaborated in assuring that the American synthesis of political, economic, and educational values embodied in her commitment to education would be largely without any problematic dimensions. The consequent need for labor market information and for mechanisms that would assure careful utilization of this data to the ends that educational investments could be judiciously made was simply not a pressing one.

Consider that since the beginning of the century we experienced rapid technological change, economic growth, an emergent shift in economic activities from the production of goods to the provision of services, two wars, and ascension to a position of world leadership, with all that such a role implies in regard to weaponry, scientific exploration, and multifaceted international involvements. The demands for educated manpower associated with the challenges and opportunities posed by these dramatic changes are by now well known, and they were translated into a very long list of decisions whose burden it was to expand higher education to a fare-thee-well!*

During the first half of the century, and perhaps until the mid-1960s, there accordingly seemed to be little reason to engage in much sophisticated long-range planning regarding higher education: an examination of population trends, coupled with extrapolations of past economic data, pointed directly to the need for more colleges and universities, more educators, more physical facilities, and more of the supporting services that would make it possible to teach the growing hordes of students whose applications innundated harried academic bureaucrats.

"Planning" efforts, such as they were in times gone by, understandably focused on the demands of individual consumers rather than on detailed economic developments that would shape the occupational structure into which degree-holders would eventually move. The most conspicuous evidence, for a very long time, pointed to the likelihood that this structure would continue to evolve so that growing, and later, massive educational inputs would be more than justified. Hardly a congressman or state legislator there was whose attention was not directed, in discussions of education, to the demands of a growing population with increasing interests in education.

Gradual and then rapid expansion of the educational apparatus was, for the most part, endorsed by the citizenry. Misgivings about the role of the academy, when they were expressed, were typically more informed by conservative political fears than by economic and theoretical reservations concerning the society's likely lines of development. Americans had not, historically, recognized any essential conflicts between an economic meritocracy and a political democracy, and they accepted a logic of income distribution according to which deservingly meritorious (which is to say better educated) individuals received higher incomes than those who had not foregone income to pursue higher education. The truth, of course, was — and is — that we are a constititutional Republic, a fact that tempered the philosophical and ideological significance of any "marginal" inequality engendered by formal higher education. Even during the Great Depression the most seriously victimized citizens expressed more misgivings about their earlier pursuit of boom-period incomes, at the expense of educations that might have earned them depression-proof jobs, than about the operation of the "system."

The statistical correlation between educational achievement and personal income had always been high in industrial America, of course, and this cold fact, above all, could be mobilized in support of basic claims made by and for education. And the interpretation of the correlation was readily available in the early chapters of any responsible (i.e., neoorthodox) economic textbook.

---

*It will be necessary, later in this chapter, to comment on the public policies that, though *remote* from educational decision-making, also had implications for manpower and therefore educational developments.

Employers and other consumers of labor services paid better-educated workers more because these citizens are worth more, which is to say they are more productive, in some considerable measure, by virtue of their educational achievements.

The consequences of these mutually reinforcing developments, and of the mensurational efforts of social scientists that helped validate a widespread consensus regarding education's legitimacy, was to establish a significant place for schooling in the minds of the citizens and, more importantly, in the minds of their policy-makers.

In these circumstances — in which statistical correlations, ideology, pragmatic values, and economic indicators all pointed in the same direction — there could be little need for questioning any of the multiple assumptions about the favorable impacts of education on the realities of the nation's development. If room at the very, very top of the socioeconomic structure was decidedly cramped, it seemed hardly doubtful that the supply of highly educated manpower fell well below the demand for professionals and leaders and for top-notch managers, both in public and private sectors.

Evidence of our extraordinary faith, in modern times, in the potency of education as an "explanatory variable" in socioeconomic analysis, finally, could be found in the central place assigned it in both the rhetoric and the reality of the efforts that were supposed to help move us, in the 1960s, from the New Frontier to the Great Society by way of the War on Poverty. Once these programs were announced, there were to be innumerable skirmishes against the educational deficiencies of the poor. If high-income earners had such increments of education as largely explained their earnings, according to a popular syllogism, then the poor must have low earnings because their educations were inadequate.

And the stuff of economic analysis provided whatever evidence was necessary to justify the crystallization of the popular view of education's role and to justify further the increasingly uncritical investment of yet more faith, and money, in education's potency. Thus, in the early and mid-sixties a number of monographs appeared in which education was held to be a major factor in economic growth through its contribution to improvements, measured by income terms, in "human capital." And the "returns" on this form of capital, both social and personal, were reported to be very impressive, indeed, when compared to returns on alternative investments.

Beyond the general predisposition to view educational investments favorably, there have been some specific stimuli: Sputnik created one kind of furor, while the idea that education should be the vehicle by which equality of opportunity would be delivered to blacks became a basic part of the conventional wisdom. In both cases education was the chosen means for achieving what many agreed were appropriate ends in the international and domestic fronts.

Numerous recent investigations, in which more direct methods than those generally used by economists in efforts to assay the character of demand for educated manpower, suggest that we have reached a point, however, at which educational planning must pay some systematic attention to labor market phenomena. Where economists typically look at data on income differences as measures of education's productivity and of the market for education, the more direct methods juxtapose census data on the population broken down by education and occupation.

In the first of these efforts, Professor R.S. Eckaus of MIT[1] compared the educational achievements of the work force, recorded in the 1940 and 1950 census reports, with the 1956 educational requirements for 4,000 jobs. The requirements were derived by translating the assignments of General Educational Development (GED) requirements made by skilled Department of Labor job analysts in 1956 to 4,000 job categories, which is to say most of the categories in the U.S. economy. His conclusion was that both "real" educational requirements and actual educational achievements were in rough balance during the 1950s. Thus, the mounting educational achievements of the population were beginning to keep pace with the growing labor force requirements for well-educated personnel who reflected technological and other changes at work in the economy. Because this analysis involved data on jobs for only one point in time, while the data on educational achievements covered two points, it was not possible to determine whether changes on the job side of the matching effort, apparently operative between 1940 and 1956, would continue to be as dramatic as they predictably would be on the achievement side.

A short time later Professors John Folger and Charles Nam reported data, in a valuable census monograph on education, that helped clarify this question to some degree. Their analysis, which was restricted to white males between the ages of 35 and 54, subdivided into the 9 major occupational groups commonly used in the decennial census, shows that "the association of education and occupation has been moderate but is declining. (Gamma = .52 in 1940, .50 in 1950, and .39 in 1960.)[2]

The investigators then sought to determine whether the demand for better-educated employees reflected an increase in supply or changes in supply reflected the stimulation of demand. Subdividing the rise in educational attainment into a component due to increases in educational attainment within occupational groups shows that upgrading within groups is by far the more important:

> Overall, about 85 per cent of the rise in educational attainment may be attributed to increased levels *within* occupations, and only 15 per cent to shifts in the occupational structure from occupations requiring less education to occupations requiring more . . . .
>
> Only at the extremes of the attainment distribution (that is for college graduates and for persons with no education) was as much as one half the change in educational attainment attributable to shifts between occuaptions.[3]

Because the occupational categories were so broad, Professors Folger and Nam, while conceding that "the educational levels of workers in various occupations do change and reflect the 'supply' of persons as well as the occupational demand," concluded that, "how much of the change reflects increased skill requirements . . . and how much is due to the availability of better-educated persons for the same jobs cannot be finally determined from these data."[4]

While the authors were cautious, in this regard, it is clear that recent increments of college graduates have spread out into the middle levels of the occupational structure. Between 1950 and 1960, the labor force gained about one-half million *more* male college graduates than were required to maintain 1950 educational attainment levels. If 1975 distributions for males remain the same as obtained in 1960, "there will be about 3.1 million more high school graduates, 850,000 more persons with some college education, and 3.3 million more college graduates than will be required."[5] Even if the upgrading trend continues within occupational groups, the possibilities of a greater rate of absorption of college graduates into the professions are not high (since the proportion is already high). The large projected increase, perforce, will have to be absorbed in "managerial, sales, clerical and some craftsmen occupations."[6]

These judgments are not intended to imply that there should be *automatic* cutbacks in efforts to provide a large number of opportunities for higher education. They do imply that we must examine carefully the economic-occupational promises that may realistically be held out to those who pursue higher education. This conclusion gains considerable support from an analysis that sought to replicate and extend the one conducted earlier by Professor Eckaus.

Thus, in the late 1960s, the author, in collaboration with Dr. Marcia K. Freedman of the Columbia University Conservation of Human Resources Project, compared the educational achievements of the work force reported in the 1950 and 1960 census with the requirements for 4,000 jobs in 1956 and 1966. The methods in this effort were substantially like those employed by Professor Eckaus, though the author's study was able to capitalize on the fact that a second assessment of job requirements (GED) had been undertaken by the Bureau of Employment Security since Professor Eckaus had completed his investigation.

In the later effort we prepared five different versions of the translations of the GED requirements (into years of schooling) assigned by Department of Labor job analysts to jobs, one each according to five more or less conservative assumptions about the meaning of the essentially qualitative GED categories. We concluded that, while the date at which an equilibrium had been reached between worker achievements and job requirements varies from one translation of GED to the next, an equilibrium had been reached at least by 1966. To be sure, there are flaws in the details of the methods used in these studies, but they do not appear to undermine the essential validity of the effort.[7]

In the same year Professor Nam, this time with Drs. Helen S. Astin and Alan E. Bayer, returned to basic census data and made careful extrapolations of the supply and demand for educated manpower.[8] These researchers report that the calculations

for a static labor force size indicate that our colleges are producing graduates at a rate that is considerably above the rate of change in the occupational structure. When labor force expansion is added to the rate of change in the occupational structure, then the rate of educational upgrading . . . is much lower in the 1960 to 1970 period, but it was substantial for the 1950 to 1960 period, and is expected to rise again to the 1950-1960 rate in the 1970-1980 period. . . .

Between 1960 and 1965, colleges produced about 900,000 more male graduates than were required for replacement and occupational growth purposes; and from 1965 to 1980, they may be expected to produce almost 1,800,000 more than are necessary.*

Hard upon the heels of the two last studies, Dr. Ann R. Miller sought to articulate the more numerous job classifications used in the *Dictionary of Occupational Titles* with those used in the census, a task like the one undertaken by my own study, mentioned above. In the process, she made comparisons of job requirements with educational achievements. But, where I worked with census data on educational achievement of workers in 1950 and 1960, and with job traits applicable to the bulk of jobs in 1956 and 1966, Dr. Miller used job data from 1966 and educational data from the sample household enumeration conducted by the Bureau of the Census in October 1966 as part of its regular Current Population Survey.[9]

Dr. Miller, after cross-tabulating GED requirements for jobs (using one translation of these requirements into years of schooling) with the more nearly contemporary data on educational achievements, writes,

For professional, technical and managerial workers, the distributions by GED and educational attainment bear some resemblance to each other, both for males and females. . . . Beyond this, however, it is hard to imagine two more dissimilar distributions. . . . If we accept the two sets of data at their face value, that is disregard the questionable elements in each, it is hard to escape the conclusion that the high level of educational attainment in this country reflects a much broader set of social values than those related to purely occupational requirements.[10]

It must be emphasized that neither the author nor those other investigators whose "direct" efforts to examine the demand for education are reported here mean to suggest that education is a bad thing. On the contrary. We may all subscribe to the "broader set of values" regarding education to which Dr. Miller refers in the above citation.

At the same time, education is costly! We spent well over $25 billion in direct outlays for higher education in 1970. Tuition rates are climbing, and the

*In fairness to the authors it should be pointed out they did not draw pessimistic conclusions from their analysis, despite the findings and comments cited here. It is the view of the authors that the costs to the nation of "shortages" of higher-educated workers are greater than those generated by what may be called the underutilization of higher education.

cold fact, mentioned earlier, that people — parents, legislators, and students — will inevitably attend to the matter of return on education can be avoided only at some considerable peril. In a pragmatic, utilitarian society, it will not do to simply affirm the proposition that education is, in and of itself, a good thing and a job forever.

The fact is that the reported returns on education and the portion of economic growth attributed to education in the initial "indirect" studies by economists may well have been exaggerated. Later studies, employing more sophisticated studies and more rigorous methods, suggest as much.[11]

The further fact is there is an urgent need for educational planners to consider labor market phenomena in order to avoid decisions that do not take account of the realities facing graduates who tend to be pushed into the academy with too many promises that the market will reward them as handsomely as it did their parents and their older brothers and, in some instances, their sisters.

The studies by Eckaus, by the author, and by Miller, with their "refined" data on job requirements, and by Folger who has used more aggregated but, still, direct data on job requirements, now cover a period from 1940 to 1966! The data based on a direct approach to the demand for educated manpower, in short, now apply to nearly 15 percent of the nation's constitutional history.

While the methods may in a number of marginal ways be deficient, they are probably without serious or substantial flaws; they are replicative and virtually reinforcing, and they give evidence that the occupational structure, compared with the educational achievements of the work force, is far more stable than has commonly been supposed.

In the absence of any assurance that the population is willing to continue to make mounting investments in higher education for overwhelmingly noneconomic reasons, it is only judicious to plan educational outlays with careful attention to the structure and functioning of the economy.

Fortunately the 14 leading representative agencies in higher education have already drawn closer together, are easily accessible in the nation's capital, and are already beginning to address themselves to the issues. And professional societies, already forced to face the facts regarding the "market" for PhD's, are also open to discussion. It should hardly prove difficult to identify a mechanism that will bring appropriate information to those ultimately responsible for educational planning through these associations.

In conclusion one may note the perils of leaving the issues unjoined. We will simply see (1) unselective cuts in educational appropriations by the several states, (2) an unselective freeze on present congressional appropriations that will either overfund or underfund particular programs, and (3) new initiatives regarding support for students, programs, and institutions that will be made *without* an eye to questions of supply and demand. It is inconceivable that higher education will be served by either a philosophy that the education business should go on as usual or one that looks only at downward changes in aggregate demand for the academy's output as an appropriate corrective. Clearly there is need for a high order of intelligent and discriminating planning if we are to avoid allocating funds, particularly for capital outlays, that lead to the needless expansion of existing facilities or to the building and staffing of new institutions both at the cost of primary and secondary education and of other needed public investments.

It is, of course, easy to overlook the obstacles to an improved articulation of educational policy with "real" manpower requirements, and four of these barriers bear special mention here. While these are interrelated they may be distinguished for analytical purposes.

The first of these inheres in the expectations of the population and the difficulties of changing these expectations over any short-run period. The fact that there is a leveling off in the demand for the number of college-level jobs does not mean that there will be a proportionate leveling off in the demand for higher education in a society in which parents, particularly, have come to regard educational credentials as job requirements.

Second, we have turned so completely to higher education in connection with occupational preparation that we have neglected the training and preparatory alternatives to job entry and occupational mobility. It is in this sense that one is tempted to regard education in recent years as something of a "training robbery."

Third, we have sought to use education in America as a vehicle for the reform of an inegalitarian society. Our too simple-minded hope was that open enrollment and similar devices would give to blacks and other victims of income maldistribution, discrimination, market imperfections, unemployment, and underemployment the same ultimate rewards parceled out to the more privileged, college-graduate population. Just to recognize the patterns of their victimization is to recognize the issues that *do* have to be joined were these population groups to share in the more general national prosperity. It simply will not do, for example, for the Department of Labor to begin, as it has begun, to recognize the limits of higher education's economic role, while the Office of Education continues to regard education as the *sine qua non* of progress for all groups. Interviews with top-level personnel in these two agencies, only a few months before this chapter was written, persuade the writer that the gulf in perceptions in this regard is widening, nor narrowing.

Finally, it is clear that we will not use the mechanism of federal aid to facilitate a reduction in the magnitude, and therefore significance, of the first three obstacles. Debates on aid to higher education in Congress make it clear that there will be only a slight shift away from institutional support to schools in favor of direct aid to students and no move whatever toward grants for other than conventional higher educational pursuits. The consequences are dreary: Educational institutions will have no real incentive to reform themselves; there will be no real pressures on higher education to discover alternatives to the prototypic four-year Harvard College model of higher learning;* and we will continue to subsidize the college and graduate work of the sons and daughters

---

*The waves of doctoral candidates who have moved into the college teaching ranks have already washed away many of the interinstitutional differences in higher education in the nation in favor of the standard Ivy League liberal arts apparatus.

of the upper middle class while letting low-income children thrash around in second-rate schools or without any job-qualifying assistance whatever.[12]

Still, for all the obstacles, it will hardly be denied that considerable forward movement could be achieved regarding the articulation of schooling and work through systematized arrangements regarding relevant information. We may infer, from one recent study, that young people *are,* in fact, responsive to information *within* the higher educational system. Thus, career choices are apparently made and unmade, on relatively short notice, *within* the scope of a four-year degree program.[13] The trick will be to provide, distribute, and interpret data that may help to broaden the capacities of young people to make more choices as between one and *another* form of postsecondary exposure. Even a little improvement on this score would help!

# 8

## LABOR MARKET INFORMATION
## FOR FEDERAL GOVERNMENT
## POLICY-MAKERS

The federal government collects more varied and complete data on labor markets than the other governments in the nation. Only a relatively small part of the "basic" table data finds its way into publication; when published, the data are presented in much less detail, usually because of sample size.[1] The published data are available to policy-makers in Congress and among Executive agencies, and, in varying degrees, unpublished data can also be obtained. Unfortunately for manpower statistics, there are no information catalogs or current data inventories. One has to search through such publications as *Employment and Earnings, The Monthly Labor Review,* and statistical appendixes to *The Manpower Report* and *The Economic Report* to find current data details. As J.E. Morton pointed out in 1965, though "they do not reflect statistical production planned or underway and ordinarily they cannot be used as a source list for the great volume of statistical data which are never published."[2]

If policy-makers, their staffs, and labor market students could more readily find out what data and what series are collected as well as available, their use of the data would be enhanced. As desirable as it would be to increase the availability of presently collected manpower and labor market statistics, we recognize that data, themselves, do not provide a basis for instructing policy decisions or for monitoring program results. Most of the data tend to be descriptive, and not analytical, providing an accumulation of figures and measurements, but little information.

Raw labor data, the collected and processed quantitative measures of wages, hours, and employment, tell little about the state of the labor market unless knowledgeable men analyze them and fit them into the framework of a theory of labor markets. An abundance of *data,* therefore, does not ensure an abundance of *information;* unfortunately it may well coexist with a scarcity of information.

Almost all policy-makers with whom we spoke complained about the lack of labor market *information*. One said, "Actually we do not need more data as much as we need more analysis of what we have already — we don't know enough about the problems to illuminate them with data." Another mentioned the frustration of "lots of available data but little information — because there is no conceptual picture into which to fit the data to trigger decision-making." One high official suggested that information always seemed to lag behind decisions and policty determination. "You have to operate on the basis of political pressures and judgements, not figures and data. They come along after the decision, but even then they're not much help, for we're off on another problem." In a round-table discussion, all the officials present agreed with the judgement of one member when he said, "The big problem is that the statistical agencies are not geared to help policy-makers. We need some changes that would provide information for policy-makers and not just simply grind out more new data."

That policy-makers find themselves supplied with more data than information should not surprise anyone. The federal government has provided considerable resources for data collection, but it has not seriously confronted the budgetary and political problems that arise in transforming data into information. The major statistical agencies suffer fewer penalties and enjoy more rewards if they focus their attention on the collection process and subordinate or even forgo analysis and interpretation of data. First, since collection of data is basic, and thus prior, to their interpretation, agency officials sensibly choose to cut back on the latter if funds are short or budgets are tight. If data are uncollected, they may be irretrievably lost, whereas study and interpretation can usually be postponed. Immediacy of information is lost, of course, but not all usefulness. With costs continually rising and appropriated funds almost always smaller than needed for ongoing collection and revision or improvement of existing techniques as well as new or improved coverage, agency officials find few resources with which to support analysis and interpretation.

We offer no solution to the problem of providing analysis of data and transforming raw statistics into information. We urge the Department of Labor, particularly the Bureau of Labor Statistics (BLS) and the Manpower Administration, to strengthen their research capability and to increase the resources devoted to analysis. More highly qualified personnel and additional funding are certainly needed. Further use should be made of contracting out analytical labor market studies to university scholars and other researchers and of fellowships awarded to nongovernment researchers for study and analysis. A fellowship program could be used to bring outstanding persons to the agencies to work for short periods — a year or more — with the regular staffs. Not only would the outside fellows enjoy an opportunity to learn fully about the data resources available, but also they would provide stimulation to and be stimulated by the staff in developing information and carrying out useful analysis of the statistics. If such a program were funded by the Department of Labor for strengthening and increasing the research effort, the cost could possibly be shared by a number of agencies that require labor market information. For example, the Department of Defense, the Department of Health, Education and Welfare, and the Council of Economic Advisers could each fund one or more fellowships for outside scholars invited to work with BLS staffs. In return, the research and analysis staffs would conduct special, particular studies of value to the contributing agencies. Or the research and analysis staff might either alternatively or in addition to the fellowship program conduct regular seminars or meetings to which outside researchers are invited for the purpose of reviewing, criticizing, and stimulating further and deeper analysis of labor market data.

An augmented research and analysis staff, continually working with and through outsiders, could serve another purpose, besides providing interpretive, policy-oriented information for government officials — that of encouraging continuous, systematic investigation of the methods of data collection and processing. The group might also provide a focal point of support for additional research, both in and out of government, into fundamentals and theory. The Gordon Report recommended, long ago, some examples of research needed then. Unfortunately, the examples are still valid. "There is need to strenghten the theoretical foundation of the unemployment concept and of seasonal adjustment procedures, and it is evident that many problems in sample design and response error remain to be solved."[3]

Further, energetic research and study are urgently needed, according to Professor Wassily Leontief, to establish, maintain, and enforce "coordinated uniform classification systems by all agencies, private as well as public."[4] Scholars and labor market analysts recognize the desirability of different measurements from different sources, but they could use the resulting data more effectively if such data could more easily be reconciled than at present. Professor Leontief complained, for example, that

> the official employment statistics cannot be related without laborious adjustments to output data, industry by industry. An unreasonably high proportion of material and intellectual resources devoted to statistical work is now spent not on the collection of primary information but on a frustrating and wasteful struggle with incongruous definitions and irreconcilable classifications.

The data-collecting agencies and a strong research and analysis staff could assist those who, at present must tirelessly adjust data and waste both time and effort in trying to bend intractable data to serve informational purposes. The research groups should provide the initial research into and then spur further agency investigations of unexplained discrepancies among closely related series. The collecting agencies in particular need to furnish more frequent or more adequate measurement of groups that account for conceptual differences. More frequent publication of information assessing comparability is certainly desirable. Periodic publication of adjusted series relevant to comparability, such as those prepared for the Gordon report, should be a regular part of the research program in labor market statistics.

The quantity and quality of labor market data have steadily improved over the decade. For the sake of efficiency in exploiting limited resources, users should be encouraged and enabled to secure as much information as possible from existing data. However, even with markedly improved utilization of the data, obvious and serious gaps would remain. Some of the most important labor market activities remain obscured because we have no measure of the variables involved. We suggest three major kinds of new data that need to be collected if government policy-makers are going to be able to both design and evaluate programs that will utilize the nation's manpower resources more effectively than in the past.

The first kind of needed data is that permitting the measurement of flows of labor within and through labor markets. As the Gordon report noted in 1962, "There is a large and continuous flow in and out of the labor force — particularly in and out of the employment component. It is apparent that information on 'gross flows' into and out of the labor force can be most useful."

It can be useful not only in helping policy-makers to measure the size of the flows but also in correcting a misleading if common view of the labor market. Relying on monthly, quarterly, or yearly averages subtly suggests a static model, with slowly changing stocks of employed and unemployed persons.

In fact, the market is exceedingly dynamic. While, in 1969, employment for the year averaged almost 78 million, the number of persons who worked during the year was nearly 92.5 million, a figure 18.5 percent larger. The average number unemployed was 2.8 million, but the total number of unemployed was 12.5 million, more than a quarter of whom experienced more than one spell of unemployment. Correcting for multiple periods of unemployment, more than three times as many persons were affected by unemployment as the average figures indicate. In the decade of the seventies, an average of 2.6 million persons can be expected to leave the labor force permanently each year, and approximately 4 million will enter. But, during *each month* this year, something like 3 million persons will probably leave their jobs and about as many will find new jobs. These estimates are rough, for turnover data are available only for the manufacturing sector and a small number of non-manufacturing industries. For much of the labor force, we have no data at all.

The differences in work experience for those employed in various industries and sectors are great. While more than three-quarters of the persons employed in the six most stable industries (railroads, other transportation, public utilities except communications, chemicals, public administration, and primary metals) work year round at full-time jobs, less than one-third in the three least stable industries (private households, agriculture, and entertainment) have similar work experience. Thus, in some industries and presumably for some occupations, the employment flows must be large. With 20 percent of the males experiencing some unemployment suffering three or more spells of unemployment in 1969 — and 13 percent of the females — a sizable portion of the unemployment problem appears to be not so much an inability to find work as having to find a job again and again — a matter of finding an acceptable job. With more timely and detailed flow data, policy-makers could better identify the failures of the market to match workers and jobs and more clearly specify the particular transition points in the labor market most needing attention.

Gross flows in and out of the labor force and the employment-unemployment flows are tabulated on a monthly basis, but they have not been published even in summary form since the early 1950s due to certain deficiencies in the data. Information about the number of persons in one month who remain in the same group next month, as well as those who move into another group, cross-classified by age, marital status, occupation, industry, and other characteristics, would be most useful. The Gordon Report recommended "that despite the deficiencies, these tabulations would be useful to research — and the publication of gross-change data [should] be resumed. Meanwhile, research should be undertaken to remedy the defects in these tabulations, or at least to assess their significance."[5]

To improve the effectiveness of manpower programs and to evaluate their worth, we need to know much more than we do presently about intra-labor-force mobility. Particularly we need to know why and in what patterns workers move among occupations, industries, and jobs as well as among geographic areas. If we could trace the characteristic flows of specific subgroups, we could comprehend the problems and better devise possible solutions for persons most subject to changes in labor force status or job opportunities.

J. E. Morton concludes that

there is ample information [read data] available currently [to shed light on intra-labor-force mobility] but only for comparing employment status in two neighboring months at a time....Even when limited to bi-monthly flow patterns, which for many purposes can be pieced together without any serious loss of validity, one can trace a great many changes. There is thus room for a great deal of descriptive and analytical effort directed to the study of mobility patterns of rather small aggregates.[6]

Further, if we are to make progress in utilizing the nation's manpower, we need much more data and information on those outside the labor force. Those persons preparing to enter the labor force, those who are prepared, potential entrants, or those who have left the labor force significantly influence the operations of the labor market and can easily determine the success or failure of manpower programs. For some problesm we probably should not separate the population into simple divisions of labor force and nonlabor force, but rather examine the spectrum of persons according to the immediacy of effect they have on the market. At least, additional study and research could help us judge how much additional data on what Morton calls the "supplemented manpower reservoir" would be of use to policy-makers.

The second kind of data especially needed is the expanded coverage of employment and wage series already widely used. The services and government sectors have grown rapidly since World War II; in 1947 they accounted for less than a quarter of nonagricultural employment, but by 1970 more than a third was on their payrolls. The industry employment breakdown for services is far from matching that of manufacturing in detail, and the employment breakdowns for government reveal hardly any details at all. Earnings and hours data for these two sectors are even more deficient. No regular series on state and local government compensation are available — only indexes of earnings in the Executive branch are published; and earnings in the services sector are scantily represented by only four three-digit industries. Another deficiency is earnings and hours data for nonproduction and supervisory employees, who are an ever increasing portion of the work force. In 1947, the number of nonproduction employees on private payrolls, 4.66 million, was equal to less than 14 percent of the production workers; by 1970, the number had risen to over 10 million, equaling more than 20 percent of the number of production workers.

The most detailed earnings and hours data are for production workers in the manufacturing sectors, but not only are they a declining part of that sector, but also manufacturing employment accounts for a continuously declining share of total private employment. In 1947, production workers made up about 84 percent of all manufacturing employment, but less than 73 percent in 1970. Nonproduction employment increased at a rate more than two and one-half times that of production employment during that period. Moreover, in 1947, manufacturing employment, both production and nonproduction, made up over two-fifths of all private employment, but only one-third in 1970. Total private employment has risen more than twice as fast as manufacturing employment since the end of World War II.

More complete coverage of the nonmanufacturing sectors, particularly services, and government and of nonproduction and supervisory employees is needed for three reasons. First, collective bargaining is increasingly becoming the mode of wage determination in these sectors and for persons in these occupations. As former Secretary of Labor George Shultz noted, "Although provision of . . . wage and other data has not eliminated strikes, it is generally conceded that accurate information, known to both sides and to the public, helps to bring about quicker and more equitable solutions."[7] Second, the nonproduction and supervisory employees exert more economic influence than their numbers alone suggest. An analysis of unpublished hourly earnings data for manufacturing available at the Council of Economic Advisers, suggests that nonproduction employees' earnings are roughly one-and-a-half to one-and-two-thirds greater than those of production workers. It also indicated that changes in earnings for nonproduction employees were often greater than those for production workers, with no obvious pattern of relationship discernible. Policies aimed at affecting the earnings of production workers may be misdirected or irrelevant if the earnings of the other workers are the true targets. Until our earnings data are extended to all sectors in greater detail, policy-makers will often be making decisions in the dark.

Third, policy-makers need some comprehensive and reliable measures of current trends in compensation, particularly in times of inflation. Recent measures, based on partial data, heavily influenced by the relatively declining manufacturing sector can seriously bias the policy-makers' understanding of the problem and the recommended solutions. As Shultz pointed out,

The most comprehensive figures on labor compensation per hour are those derived on a quarterly basis from the national income accounts, for all persons in the private sector. They provide very useful information because they tell us not only what has happened to total compensation per hour, but also what has happened to labor cost per unit of output and prices. Statistics of this comprehensive nature are needed in establishing a case for anti-inflation policies, as well as in appraising their effectiveness. But few people, even among economists, know of their existence, and they rarely make front page news. Moreover, it is sometimes difficult to reconcile their movements with the other information . . . much of which is more up to date. These discrepancies raise questions as to whether the global estimates adequately reflect what is currently going on at the bargaining table or in the market place.[8]

Better and wider coverage of the service and government sectors with data on nonproduction earnings would provide a check on the national income data and add to our knowledge about current wage levels.

The staff and members of the Council of Economic Advisers have indicated, both to the Gordon committee and to more recent investigators, that one of the most urgent statistical needs is for better data on hours worked in *all* major sectors of the economy. The reasonableness and sufficiency of price changes cannot be indicated unless changes in industry productivity and unit costs are available. Industry-by-industry data are especially needed, in view of the long-term, continuing interest of the federal government in some kind of incomes policy. Over the past decade, Democratic and Republican administrations have found it desirable to seek to limit wage increases to increases in the national productivity rate; with little or no data on industry productivity, however, they have been hampered in evaluating price developments.

A third kind of data needed for policy-makers is more disaggregated measures of earnings, employment, and unemployment. Of particular importance is improvement in the labor-force reports on regional, state, and local labor market characteristics. Federal programs are often geared to activities at these levels, yet the labor market reports seldom supply the detail and reliability required. The size and complexities of the economy and the fact that Congress is especially sensitive to local problems, allocating millions of dollars to programs with decided local impacts, affirm the need for much effort in developing better labor market information than we have at present. If such information were available, it is likely that policy-makers could more clearly identify the most troublesome problem areas and design programs specifically for them; the result could be a significantly more efficient effort in improving the labor market's operation.

If reliable disaggregated data are to be made available, the Current Population Survey (CPS) operation will have to be enlarged and probably the number of questions will have to be increased. The Gordon report recommended, nearly ten years ago, that the CPS sample be increased tenfold. The cost of such an increase would be substantial and should be weighed against the cost of attempting to secure more detailed data from present sources. The cost and feasibility of matching existing CPS data with those collected from other sources, such as Internal Revenue Service tax returns or the Social Security records, should be thoroughly explored as possible alternative sources of more disaggregated and geographically specific information.

Besides disaggregating labor market data on a regional or local basis, policy-makers need more detailed breakdowns by occupations. The changes in occupations have probably been among the biggest and most significant in the labor force, though we know relatively little about the details of the shift. Between 1947 and 1970 the number of white-collar workers rose by almost 18 million, an increase of 88 percent. That was almost five times faster than the increase in the number of blue-collar workers. Among the white-collar workers, the fastest growing group was the professional, technical, and kindred workers; who nearly tripled in number. The shift to higher-qualified more highly paid occupations in the labor force has had effects on the economy and the operation of the labor market that we cannot adequately detail, given the lack of available data.

The quality of labor required for jobs and the kinds of skill competences used by various industries are recognized as factors to be carefully considered in programs affecting employment. To understand the effects of technological change, we must understand in considerable detail mismatches between job vacancies and unemployment and the contributions of schooling, training and manpower programs, and occupational shifts and mixes. At present we know relatively little about current changes in the number of workers employed in each important occupation and almost nothing about current changes in the occupational structure or mixes within industries. The currently published occupational series do not present much detail. Among professional and technical workers, for example, employment is given only for medical and other health teachers (except college) and others. Compensation by occupation is available yearly, but not on a current basis and not on a basis comparable to earning data for production workers.

Another major labor market change, the increasing number of working women, makes desirable more detailed data on women's earnings, occupations, and industrial location. The number of women in the labor force has nearly doubled from 1947 to 1970, with the participation rate rising from less than 32 percent to over 43 percent. Women average lower pay and higher unemployment than men. More detailed data could help identify causes and possible remedies for these situations, and to what extent they might be explained by differences in employment mix of men and women, by differences within the same occupation, and by differences within the same industry. Similar questions about the conditions of minority group workers might also be explored. Once such data are available, policy-makers will have the opportunity to formulate more realistic policies than at the present and to monitor their effectiveness.

As policy-makers become more concerned with the utilization of manpower and consider the quality of labor, they will require more disaggregated data. These will be expensive to collect, but the cost of collection should not be considered by itself. If the data contribute to increased returns because government programs are more relevant to the problems at which they are directed and funds are more efficiently spent, the net costs may not be nearly as great as they now appear. Of course, the first responsibilities of the data collecting agencies is to help the policy-makers use existing data more effectively than at present. We have indicated that improvement can be made in this way and should receive top priority.

# CONCLUSIONS
# AND RECOMMENDATIONS

# 9

## TOWARD A "COMPREHENSIVE" LABOR MARKET INFORMATION SYSTEM

### THE NATURE OF A "COMPREHENSIVE SYSTEM"

We can now return to our opening consideration of the meaning of the word "comprehensive" when applied to any information system. In light of the richness and variety of information, the enormous number of users and uses, and the almost infinite mix of characteristics required (which have only been highlighted in Part II), the word "comprehensive" must not be taken too literally. It would, in fact, probably be better to avoid using it altogether. A *"multipurpose" labor market information system* might be a more realistic term.

The situation is highly reminiscent of the enthusiasm of the early steps of information systems in business organizations, when the ambitious term "total information system" began to appear in the literature and in the conversations of high-level planners. It, fortunately, did not take long for reality to catch up with, and deflate, the optimistic visions.

Contrasting the size, scope, and complexity of a labor market information system with that of even the largest and most diversified single corporation does more than arouse proper humility in dealing with the former. The experiences of the corporate systems designers have taught us that the construction of a complex information system cannot be tackled as a one-time effort in which the whole system is carefully designed in final form and then implemented as a package. Rather, it is a long, continuous process in which sections, or subsystems, are tackled and implemented. Information systems, moreover, are rarely, if ever, started from scratch. Much information is already being collected, processed, and used at any stage when a new design is called for.

This is clearly the case with information about labor markets. Considerable amounts of data are in use, and many of these will necessarily form basic units within any new labor market information system design. An important stage in system design, therefore, involves the examination and evaluation of existing information sources. At this stage every effort is made to "clean up" the already collected data and, by standardizing definitions, classifications, and categorizations as far as possible, to improve their comparability with other series. This sort of effort is already being carried out, both in the Department of Labor and in the Statistical Standards Office in the Office of Management and Budget. At this point, a review of the types of labor market information currently available is in order.

## THE NATURE OF PRESENTLY AVAILABLE INFORMATION

Excluding the labor market information implicit in the "external system" of Chapter 2 (e.g., the activities of tariff, tax, transportation, and a host of other agencies), the bulk of the formal, direct labor market information available to the participants in the labor market, primarily on the national level, is published by the Bureau of Labor Statistics (BLS) in conjunction with the Census Bureau, and these are summarized in the annual BLS publication *Major Programs.* We have omitted for our purposes the series on injury statistics and on prices and living conditions and included a summary tabulation of these series and their major uses (as given in *Major Programs)* in the Appendix.

In dealing with the conceptual framework of a labor market information system, we are less concerned with the *listing* of existing bodies of data than with an examination of their formats and uses. Accordingly our discussion will focus on two general issues: the *form* of data presentation and the *needs* of the data's major users.

### The Form of Information: Standard Reports vs. Special Inquiry

The finished products of the programs we have been describing appear in general as a series of published and disseminated reports. It is important to distinguish between the published standard reports and the data base from which they are generated. One of the major contributions of the computer, aside from its high speed and capacity, has been its ability to divorce the report publications format from the data collection and storage.

With this new capability at hand, an information system can deliver a wide range of outputs. At one extreme of this range is the ability to produce *standardized* reports and summaries on a predetermined and repetitive basis. At the other extreme, the information system can deliver specific responses to particular requests and deal with different users' problems that are nonrepetitive, nonstandard for all users or unanticipated in nature.

It seems clear that the broader the range of users and uses relying on any information system, the less likely are standardized reports to meet all their requirements and, conversely, the more likely is there to be a large demand for the "special request" capability of the system. Our previous discussion of the extremely wide range of users and uses inherent in a labor market information system inevitably suggests that the future effectiveness of this sytem will greatly depend on its ability to handle "special requests." Yet the bulk of the existing data summarized in the Appendix is presented in the standard table format. Such a format will become, in our opinion, increasingly ineffective, and we firmly believe, therefore, that the suppliers of labor market information should move away from conventional, tabular publication of standardized reports and towards the provision of specific information tailored to the requests of individual users. The Department of Labor is of course aware of this need and does make special tapes available on request. The problem here becomes one of informing potential users as to what is available and how to use it. The solution of this special kind of information problem will not be provided by the mailing of conventional bulletins but requires a broadly based and continuing effort on the part of the dispensers of this kind of information.

## USERS OF INFORMATION AND THEIR NEEDS

A more substantive review of the uses of existing data sources as described in the official language of *Major Programs* and in our probes leads to the conclusion that these sources are of least service to the *direct* participants in the job market. They are of more use to the various intermediaries, particularly to planners at the macro-level of activity, and are also indispensable to the academic or academically oriented researcher. Nevertheless, labor market intermediaries and researchers would also benefit greatly from any improvement in the availability of data, particularly in response to specific requests.

We can summarize at this point the information needs of the participants in the labor market information system and against this background furnish recommendations for improvement in existing information.

### Direct Participants

Looking inside the job market itself — that is, the point at which potential employee and job vacancy are matched — we can briefly summarize the information requirements of both sides in the following characteristics. We have seen that for the direct participants information must be extremely "fresh" or up to date and must provide great detail and richness about both employee and job. Quantitative information, while important, is only a portion of the full needs of both employer and employee. It is difficult to list in advance the many things a particular employee would like to know about a job aside from such numerical data as wage rate, number of paid vacations, and hours worked. Similarly complex and detailed is the information an employer would like to have about any potential employee. The higher the occupational level, the greater the richness of the information needs of both parties and, to a marked extent, the less determining is the quantitative component of it. For this reason it is not surprising to discover that friends and relations are the most commonly used sources of information for potential employees. They possess what is needed: a great wealth and particularity of information about a relatively small number of job openings. For this reason, we have some reservations about the ability of computer-based data banks to substitute for all types of job-matching procedures.

## INTERMEDIARIES

For the intermediaries we have identified in the system, on the other hand, labor market information is needed for both planning and control.

The nongovernment intermediaries on both sides will generally rely in part on public and governmental sources for the data needed for planning. While, for control purposes, firms will ordinarily use their own internal reporting systems in evaluating their own performance and arriving at decisions for corrective action, they will on the other hand rely on public sources, at least in part, for the data and analysis needed for planning.

From a manpower point of view, for example, planning by employers should entail the use of quite specific forecasts of the supply and demand conditions in local labor markets by occupation and industry. The well-known limitations of such forecasts have however made firms cautious in using them. The Department of Labor and individual state and local agencies have devoted considerable effort to coping with these problems, but increasing experience has led to a heightened awareness of the limitations of existing techniques.

Manpower planning is a relatively new and not very well-developed activity in most large firms. The major concern of employers at present is manpower administration, a concern that tends to focus on control. Looking to the future, however, most observers predict that for a variety of reasons manpower planning will have to assume greater importance, particularly on the part of large employers. This heralds new and greater demands on public information systems.

### Government

The government as intermediary is in a somewhat special position. It requires large amounts of public information for both planning and control. Congress, for example, must initiate and fund programs, as well as evaluate their effectiveness. Here we face the full range of information characteristics, and their conflicting nature for planning and control purposes.

A major impetus behind the request of Congress that "a comprehensive labor market information system" be set up is the concern of legislators that they cannot, on the basis of informational resources presently made available by governmental agencies, judge the value of past programs effecting labor markets or frame programs for the future based on adequate foreknowledge of possible problems and the steps that might be taken to meet them.

Melvin Anshen has graphically described the problem that faces Congress. Take for example "the problem of budgeting for activities designed to alleviate poverty and rooted unemployment." First of all, Congress is told that these are "complex phenomena traceable to such varied causes as economic recession, technological change, obsolete skills, insufficient education, racial prejudice, immobility of labor, and inadequate supply of information on distant job opportunities." The remedies suggested are "equally varied." "The only significant issue," Anshen concludes, "is whether the answer rests on intuition . . . or a budget system that presents relevant information so organized as to contribute to rational analysis, planning, and decision-making."[1]

We may usefully follow Anshen another step and underline a point made earlier in Chapter 2. A comprehensive labor market information system, should be designed, among other purposes, to provide the needed data for Congress and the Executive agencies to cope with the impact of the federal budget on the labor market. At the same time, however, it should be remembered that even a "comprehensive" labor market information system is itself only part of a larger informational system, which provides the framework for the trade-offs that determine the final budget.

In addition to the need for budgeting and planning, there is an increasing awareness of the necessity for evaluation and control of government programs; reference has been made in Chapter 3 to the evaluation functions of Manpower Automated Reporting Systems (MARS) and Employment Security Automated Reporting Systems (ESARS). The Urban Institute study *Federal Evaluation Policy*,[2] by J.S. Wholey and others, puts the matter succinctly:

> The most impressive finding about the evaluation of social programs in the federal government is that substantial work in this field has been almost nonexistent . . . .
>
> The impact of activities that cost the public millions, sometimes billions, of dollars has not been measured. One cannot point with confidence to the difference, if any, that most social programs cause in the lives of Americans.[3]

The reports of the Olympus Research Corporation[4] underline the same point and stress further the importance of follow-up data, without which there can be no real evaluation of the worth of a program. Ideally, according to Wholey,

> Evaluation should examine policies and programs from the broadest national level down to specific operations of projects at the local level, including their impact on individuals. A range of types of evaluation is needed to focus on these different targets . . . .
> . . . Evaluation findings should be widely disseminated and put to use. This will be a self-reinforcing process. When top policy leaders — whether in the White House, Bureau of the Budget, Congress, departments or program manager offices — are seen to give or withhold funds and to expand or alter program content as a result of evaluation, the art of systematic assessment is bound to be enhanced.

A final warning on the limits of evaluation:

Not everything one might want to investigate in federal programs can be evaluated . . . . It is essential, therefore, to know the limits of what evaluation can accomplish. Improving methodologies also is a vital function of a comprehensive evaluation system.[5]

Any attempt at evaluating the enormous range of manpower activities by direct, centralized, national control of individual programs implies an impossible load of detailed and frequent information. One cannot visualize an information system capable of providing such control needs centrally.

The answer here lies not in elaborating the information system, but in decentralizing control to units closer to the scene of performance and in superimposing a broader level of controls over these units. A hierarchy of controls is required with a reasonable load of detailed information at each level to permit effective monitoring of performance at the level below it. Many effective models, and considerable operating experience with them, are available in large business corporations, particularly among conglomerates and other highly diversified organizations.

## SUMMARY OF CONCLUSIONS

A number of broad conclusions need to be highlighted before we proceed to spell out concrete recommendations for an improved labor market information system in our next and final chapter.

- Very many information users, besides the direct participants in a diverse mix of labor markets, make a multitude of decisions, which, *in toto,* give shape, direction, and size to this market.
- A broad variety of models, theories, and frameworks guide those decision-makers in attempting to cope with an extremely complex reality.
- Depending on the model selected, and the decision-maker's view of his mission, what constitutes "good" information becomes an almost unique set of specifications of information characteristics for each user and use.
- The characteristics of information required for even short-run decisions by the direct participants in the labor market are highly varied. Depending on which segment of the market (occupational, geographic, or institutional) is considered, varying emphases of characteristics are called for. Personal user perception and values affect the proper characteristics mix for any given employee or employer.
- Existing published data, although voluminous and extensive, often fail to meet the specific needs of decision-makers and are frequently ignored altogether. There appears to be relatively little clamoring for more or additional "general purpose" data from the intermediaries we have examined. This may be a result of either unsophisticated planning by the intermediaries or of the lack of publicly distributed data that they find useful. It is most likely a combination of both, in an interacting cycle of cause and effect.
- A general impression, frequently conveyed by government policy-makers but echoed by many other intermediaries, is that "we are not short of data, but of information." Major problems center on the selection, processing,

and presenting of the information needed, rather than the availability of the basic units of data from which it is constructed.

- Most frequent criticism of existing data is not directed at their volume, but rather at their lack of comparability and consistency across series and time spans. The need for standardized classifications, uniform definitions, and consistent statistical treatment has been emphasized for many years now. It is still an important need for data users.

- Government-based data are only one of a variety of sources used by participants and intermediaries in the labor market. They are often supplemented by other data, generated internally, by other sources, or through services that combine government and other data for specific applications.

- Until information and knowledge go through a valuation process similar to what takes place in a market, there does not seem to be any clear-cut way by which we can say whether this or that bit of information or knowledge, as compared to any other bit, should be collected, analyzed, and disseminated. It is for this reason that, wherever possible, data and information should undergo a pricing (or shadow-pricing) process. We should know what are the full costs and marginal costs associated with various data-collecting, analyzing, and disseminating programs. Those charged with decisions about the extension or contraction of information programs should also know what the information is worth to its users. This is not to say that information should actually be sold. Whether this is desirable in any particular case is an entirely different question.

When one has this background of knowledge about the supply and demand curves for various kinds of information, and about the prices that would be generated by such supply and demand conditions, it then becomes possible to ask more difficult questions about the social costs and social benefits of various kinds of information, as well as their private costs and benefits.

It is against this background that the recommendations in the next chapter are pointed.

## RECOMMENDATIONS

### An Idealized "Comprehensive" Labor Market Information System

We can now assess the implications of our study and draw some conclusions about the task of reshaping and improving the existing labor market information system. We can best present these in terms of a series of progressive steps toward an "idealized" future system. We will begin by briefly describing the earmarks of an ideal system, realizing that such a system is a shifting goal. It is really only a perception at present, but it is needed to give guidance and direction to intermediate steps.

An idealized, "multipurpose" labor market information system would consist of large-scale, random-access data banks, containing all the detailed transactions and data bits collected by all government agencies as well as other data-gathering organizations. The stored data would be classified by standardized, consistent classifications and would be comparable in terms of time base, units of measurement and data source. Any participant or intermediary in the labor market would have direct access to these data banks, with some provision for the security of confidential information and protection of privacy (however these values are defined at the time). Each user would be able, therefore, to draw on the stored data, process them in accordance with his own analytical needs, and interpret their results as he sees fit. Users would spell out their own information needs to deal with specific decisions confronting them. Some of these needs would be met by repetitive, periodic analyses and reports scheduled at desired frequencies. Others would be one-time or special-purpose analyses made on demand.

The ideal system would be partly self-supporting financially, with some users paying for the services rendered in proportion to their costs, although public policy may require that other users or uses be subsidized. While we recognize the difficulty in estimating costs and in setting a "fair" price for information, we believe the effort should be made. The importance of the charge (direct or subsidized) for services rendered goes beyond the desirability of a balanced budget. It gives true meaning to the basic notion of the value of information. Users will, presumably, obtain only the information that their own cost-benefit analysis will justify, thus, ideally, avoiding waste of resources and ensuring economic efficiency of the system. Similarly, such charges will provide a concise and precise means of identifying all system users and the extent of their usages. It would also, presumably, provide a direct incentive to the system's operators to cater, and be responsive, to the needs of its major users. It should be noted that charges for services do not preclude the government's subsequently subsidizing any users or institutions deemed worthy of public support.

The system should, further, be able to service a large variety of users, in response to their relative sophistication and equipment capability in data processing. Thus users with extensive in-house equipment and advanced technical skills may simply use (and pay for) the retrieval of specific data inputs from the storage banks. They may request these data by direct access or by acquiring a tape or disc pack from the system's operators. At the other extreme a user may describe his needs to the system technicians, who will then proceed to program, process, and print the requested report. This user would be charged for the technicians' time and the processing cost.

A system of this kind would make full use of the flexibility of electric data processing, be able to meet individual decision-makers' needs, and be self-sustaining at that volume of operations that justifies information costs. It would contain qualitative as well as quantitative data. Such a system, however, will take many years to realize and will call for the solution of a multitude of technical and political problems.

The road to the ideal system briefly highlighted above is, indeed, a long and tortuous one. It must be traveled, however, by a series of discrete "bites," a series of projects dealing with the major components of the total system. Experience with business information systems suggests that an effective approach is one that attempts a dual attack: "bottom-up" and "top-down" — that is, the selection of projects at the lower levels of application, which may be seen as the "building blocks" of the over-all system, while simultaneously work is done on high-level applications that utilize system-wide aggregations and permit some experimentation in coordinating information from various subsystems. The former projects typically provide some short-run, tangible payoffs as well as experience in meeting the needs of users at the micro or operational level. The latter projects permit some experimentation in determining the shape of the over-all system and responding to the needs of users at the macro or policy-formulating levels.

We recommend a similar dual-level approach by the Department of Labor to the implementation of the labor market information system conceptualized here. We will outline a proposed project at the operating, or local, level as well as a series of steps to be followed at the policy-making or national level. These will be presented successively below. In addition we will make some general recommendations for increasing the availability and usefulness of information for labor market participants.

## POLICY PROPOSAL ON THE LOCAL LEVEL: PILOT PROJECT

Direct participants, as well as intermediaries in local labor markets, require information of considerable detail and qualitative richness relating to a rather narrowly defined geographic area. In addition, there is a great degree of diversity in local labor markets. The pluralistic nature of American life and institutions results in considerable diversity among localities and regions. Political, social, and institutional arrangements vary significantly across the nation. Program administrators in New York City operate in a very different environment from their opposite numbers in Atlanta, Los Angeles, or even Philadelphia — only 90 miles distant.

Local labor markets, therefore, present a unique set of problems both in terms of user needs and the available information resources and channels. An effective labor market information system must, thus, be made up of a large number of subsystems, each focusing on its local market. At the same time, each of the local components must truly act as a subsystem, in the sense that it provides useful inputs to the larger over-all system.

The benefits of a local labor market information system to all its participants — employees, employers, and corporate manpower planners, educational and training facilities, public and private employment agencies, and local program administrators — are widespread. In addition, a coordinated local information pooling project will serve to explore the benefits of voluntary, cooperative, data sharing.

There is a general feeling among nongovernmental participants in labor markets that further legislative or coercive measures for data gathering and reporting will not prove as effective as voluntary, *quid pro quo* exchanges. Private employers, for example, would probably gladly report nonconfidential information in their files, if they felt they were getting some direct benefits for their trouble — benefits, typically, in the form of better data about their local labor markets, which they themselves do not possess and which would be operationally useful. Voluntary exchanges, therefore, would open up entry into many data bodies that could not be effectively tapped by legislation or regulation.

Similarly, freer exchange of data between the several local participants would reduce duplication of effort considerably. Preliminary inquiries show that, not only in the private sector but also in many govermental agencies, the same data are needlessly collected and stored in several sources. In some cases duplication is a result of ignorance of the existence of parallel sources, in others of the lack of desire or ability to exchange information between sources.

Finally, there is a great need for formalizing and structuring much of the informal and haphazard exchanging of information that currently permits the system to work. Many local participants do draw on each others' knowledge and data when special needs arise or when specific projects give birth to temporary and makeshift exchange arrangements. We argue for formalization and stabilization of such interchanges, and not only for reasons of efficiency and cost savings. We firmly believe that informal systems do not adapt rapidly enough to changing demands on them and will not to the inevitable restructuring of labor market practices and institutions that can be foreseen in the decade ahead.

In contrast to the advantages and objectives of closely coordinated local information systems listed above, it is well to consider briefly the current situation in the usual metropolitan labor markets. Typically large bodies of information on manpower, employment, and related issues are dispersed among many participants in the labor market. Much of this information may be of interest only to a few or be properly classified as confidential or proprietary. Some portion of it, however, would be extremely useful and greatly welcomed by many of the major participants in the labor market, particularly those who spend considerable amounts of money and effort in data collection, assembly, and analysis.

Yet, despite the efforts involved, each participant confronts gaps and deficiencies in information and rarely knows how to go about closing these gaps. In some cases, the desired information may simply be unavailable, or at least not economically available. In many instances, however, the needed data (or some very close surrogate) may be found in another source's files. Besides economic constraints, data circulation is often restricted by political consideration. To the extent that the possession of information implies power or independence from outside control, there may be an inherent reluctance to release it.

We believe that the often haphazard nature of information exchange in local labor markets is primarily the result of four major factors:

(1) There is no formal mechanism by which data sources can be located, inventoried, and categorized. No systematic effort has been made, to our knowledge, to search out, develop, or build up an inventory of the major information resources in any local market.

(2) Even for known data sources, there are no formal exchange and distribution procedures between interested parties. The occasional makeshift arrangements put together by one or two data users are a far cry from the needed formalization of policies, procedures, and major distribution channels for effective interchange.

(3) There has been no careful analysis of the cost and benefits of a cooperative data-sharing program to the participants. A *quid pro quo* voluntary system, moreover, requires the identification of the major information needs, availabilities, and gaps of participants as its exchange foundation.

(4) Among the many agencies and firms that would participate in a data-sharing program, there is no single institution clearly identifiable as the coordinator or clearing house for the system. A variety of coordinative functions, coupled with some procedural authority, would almost certainly be required at the hub of a local information system. Ideally, again, such a coordinating agency would be accepted voluntarily by all participants on the basis of its contribution to their individual needs. A search for means of

111

overcoming these four major difficulties should, therefore, be the first order of business.

## Pilot Project: Recommended Approach

We have repeatedly emphasized the pluralistic nature of the local labor market and the advantages of voluntarism in its coordination. Our proposal is, therefore, structured on a "consortium" approach. It seeks to draw all the major participants into both the design and the implementation of a local information system. Implementation must, obviously, be the result of this initial effort and cannot be spelled out *a priori.*

We propose that the Department of Labor support and fund one or more pilot projects in which the research team would draw on representatives of the several groups of major participants in the selected market. These would typically include major employers; governmental agencies involved in manpower, training, employment, and data collection programs; major education facilities (private and public, elementary and advanced); leading unions; and local government administrators. It would be useful to include some subunits of agencies dealing with housing, welfare, transportation, and other major social issues with important labor market implications. The team would, in effect, combine research with a leadership and coordination function among the future components of the system. Let us outline an approach to this task before returning to some of the mechanics and logistics of the pilot project.

The first objective of the research should be better use and delivery of *existing* information. The point of view should clearly emphasize getting more effective use from what is already available, *before* going out to collect or generate new information.

The essential initial step, therefore, is an inventorying of the major bodies of data available within the local market. This implies locating the firms, agencies, and institutions that are potentially the principal sources and users of labor market information. Once these are located, their data sources should be roughly classified and catalogued in terms of subject, scope, detail, frequency, etc. Consideration should be given at this stage to the confidential or proprietary nature of any source data and the level of aggregation that could make such data publishable.

The other side of the coin involves determining the informational needs of the principal participants. Existing information gaps need to be both inventoried and categorized, so that a search for "matches" with available data sources can be carried out.

Both facets of the survey of sources and gaps must, of necessity, rely heavily on the cooperation and support of the several participants. A by-product of the survey stage should, therefore, be the building up of interest and willingness to share. The consortium approach should be continuously emphasized in both planning and action. The research team must apply considerable ingenuity and creativity in locating potential cost savings through elimination of duplication and in matching each participant's needs for information with other available sources in the system.

**112**

Once the survey, inventory, and classification are accomplished, the research should proceed to the design of an ongoing, integrated local information system.

At the simplest or lowest level of investigation, the local consortium would do nothing more than publish a catalogue or inventory listing of all major information sources in the system, to whom they may be available, and under what conditions. Such an arrangement would serve simply to inform all participants of what data are available and leave it to them to arrange for, or negotiate, exchanges.

The consortium could move further and develop some standard classification and definitions, so that greater compatibility could be achieved in different data sources. Any data falling within such "standardized" categories would then be readily usable by any two or more sharers. It is realized that complete standardization and compatibility is an extremely demanding job and is not likely to be achieved quickly in a voluntary consortium. On the other hand some standardization can be achieved by agreement, particularly when it requires relatively minor changes in the practices of its collectors.

The consortium could move a step further and design specific channels, policies, and procedures for the routine interchange of information among participants as well as some ground rules for special-purpose projects or surveys. Similarly the consortium would have a wide range of choices in selecting a coordinating institution or clearing house. Such a clearing house could serve as the "library," "publisher," or "computer center" for consortium information exchanges.

It is obviously much too early to discuss the possible institutional arrangements for coordination and clearing. Our study, and other research in the field, however, points to one possible agency as coordinator, the United States Employment Service (USES).

### Pilot Project: USES as Local Systems Coordinator

Much has been written and argued about the proper mission for USES.[1] Against this background, the selection of the USES office as the coordinator or clearing house of the local labor market information system might prove an effective strategy on several sources. Serving as the system's clearing house could well help USES expand its range of vacancy listings by bringing it into closer contact with employers, guidance counselors, and training establishments — all highly desirable developments. Furthermore USES has a core of experienced personnel and represents a reasonably "neutral ground" between the private sector, and local, state, and regional government agencies.

### Pilot Project: Proposed Action Steps

We recommend the launching of one or more projects as one of the early efforts of the Department of Labor in pursuing the development of a labor market information system. The location of pilot projects deserves careful attention. We believe that New York City should be included in any such pilot project for a variety of reasons.

The New York City labor market is the largest, most heterogeneous, and most complex in the country. In addition, major participants in the New York City labor market have shown a keen interest in improving its information base, and some preliminary studies and research projects have already been launched. Thus, some of the ingredients for the pilot study are already available. Finally, New York provides a variety of high-grade personnel, both in research and supporting functions, to ensure professional competence. A New York City project could well be coupled with projects in several other cities. A relatively homogeneous labor market, such as is found in Pittsburgh, might provide good contrast to New York City's diverse occupational and population mix.

For each model project selected, a research team should be nominated. The team should be directed to establish a task force and an advisory committee, representing the several participants in the system under study. The contacts and good offices of the U.S. Department of Labor as well as of the city governments concerned should be used to get maximum cooperation at all possible levels.

The research attack on the problem has already been discussed in the preceding section. It is, therefore, perhaps best to conclude with a brief statement on what might be the major contents of the report of the research teams. It should describe the analysis and findings of its surveys, propose an operating system for the locality selected, suggest the mechanism for its maintenance as well as its funding, and outline an implementation schedule.

It should be noted that the project should aim at a double payoff. First, it will design an operational system for the location selected. Equally important, it will serve as a model for other areas. We are convinced that local differences would make each system largely unique. The model project will, however, serve as a prototype for the methodology and attack on a complex problem. For this reason we suggest that an important part of the project report will focus on the methods used, experiences gained, and frustrations encountered in the pilot survey and design.

### Pilot Project: Expected Benefits

We are convinced, in conclusion, that the development of a local labor market information system based on a consortium approach deserves high priority. For members of the labor force, it should lead to a reduction in search time between jobs and increased opportunities for upgrading. For the employer and corporate manpower planner, there should result a reduction in the costs of hiring, more reliable data on salaries, wages, and hours in the local market, an improved ability to plan for on-the-job training through improved forecasting of skills in short supply, and improved data of the kind required for compliance with Office of Economic Opportunity regulations.*

---

*This last has become for some major employers an increasingly difficult and delicate informational problem.

Little need be said of the importance of good local market information to employment agencies, both public and private. It is their stock in trade and the very foundation of their business. The value of good local information to local manpower program administrators should be equally apparent, particularly with the current acceleration of revenue-sharing. A widely based consortium should also increase the ability of local manpower administrators to incorporate in their programs the important but often ignored manpower effects of a wide spectrum of programs in the areas of highway construction, transportation, and housing.

Improved data should permit the more accurate projection of future trends in the demand for skills on the part of educational and training facilities and the development of more realistic curriculums by them. Increased coordination among these agencies should lead to a considerable reduction in duplication and an elimination of training deficiencies. The increased availability of fuller local data to such facilities should also help to close a major informational gap: the lack of understanding of the world of work by young people.

Another benefit of the local consortium system can be understood only with reference to our argument put forth in Chapter 9 that there cannot be an effective national centralized control of individual manpower programs, but that there should be a hierarchy of controls. The information generated by the local consortium has the required degree of detail, flexibility, and immediacy for use by that part of the control system — the decentralized control units — that is closest to the local manpower programs. Moreover, this information, properly processed, summarized, and integrated can provide much of the statistical base essential to effective control at higher levels.

## THE APPROACH ON THE NATIONAL LEVEL: STEPS FOR IMPROVING INFORMATION HANDLING

Parallel to the introduction of a labor market information pilot project at the local level, we recommend some changes in the form and availability of the information furnished to users at the national levels. These changes are designed to improve the quality of information provided to those major users probed in Chapters 4 through 8 with special emphasis on the federal government policy-maker. We present these as a series of progressive steps moving from the existing to the "idealized" system sketched out at the beginning of this chapter. Some of these are already being tried or used in varying degrees.

### Step One: Improving Existing Data

Starting with the existing government-based data series, early emphasis should be on "better," rather than "more." The temptation to collect more or new raw data should be resisted except where clear need is established. The attitude indicated in Chapter 8 should be one of "We already have more raw material than we know what to do with." Efforts should be directed at improving the quality, comparability, and compatibility of the data now being collected. First, useless or obsolete data series should be dropped. Over the years, series are added in response to some need but are usually not eliminated once that need is passed.

Next, standardization of classifications and statistical procedures should be accelerated. Little need be added to the familiar arguments here. Finally, improved availability of data can be achieved by the creation of a central index of data series available from several sources, accompanied by full documentation of the classifications, statistical procedures, and dates of each source. As a somewhat longer-run effort, such indexing and documentation should also be extended to major data sources *outside* the federal government.* Lessons learned in developing "consortium" local projects, as proposed earlier, would prove extremely valuable here, too.

now examine the stages in the publication and dissemination of these data. In what follows, we have in mind primarily the needs of national policy-makers, but it will be clear from our discussion that a number of our recommendations apply as well or even more directly to labor market participants on other levels. The underlying trend should be one of moving from the emphasis on "universal," "all-purpose," "something-for-everybody" publication toward increased emphasis on special-purpose, select-audience reports.

## Step Two: Moving Toward More Specialized Publication

As a first stage, a few major categories of users should be identified and selected. The major intermediaries discussed in this volume make a logical starting place for the search. For each of these, a detailed survey of information needs should be conducted, probably through a combination of mail survey and interviews in depth. Based on these needs, a revised set of published reports can be designed. Their format, content, and frequency of updating can be presented to the potential users in the category and can then be modified in accordance with their reaction. Modified reports can be published and distributed to users in that category.

In a sense the current work on computerized job-matching banks represents an application of the principle we are proposing above. These banks are, in effect, specialized data assemblies for selected, regional users. Nor need the principle of charging or "shadow pricing" for such services be ignored. If the systems prove effective, service charges may be levied on employers or debited to USES in the form of interagency charges.

At this point it is perhaps appropriate to repeat an earlier warning. While the job-matching systems may improve the efficiency of job market transactions, they should not be seen as the panacea or even the central effort of an improved information system.

---

*We recognize that great care must be exercised to avoid invasion of confidentiality not only on general moral grounds but also because this can be a self-defeating process when information sources dry up or decrease in reliability, as a consequence.

A second stage, or refinement, of the select-audience report could be the provision of *a choice of output* for the subscribing user. In addition to printed reports, users may elect to receive magnetic tapes containing the same data. Such users could then process the data, on their own equipment, in any variations of analysis they may elect. Again, a service charge, reflecting the added cost of tape preparation could be levied.

We believe that, after some experience is gained in both designing and "marketing" select-audience reports, their number and diversity should continue to expand.* A succession of users and uses can be tackled in an order of priorities determined by the level of the demand and importance of the user in the labor market process. It is hoped, also, that no significant addition to resources will be called for. As the number of select-user reports increases, there should be a compensating reduction in the volume and distribution of the "universal" publications published by the Department of Labor.

## Step Three: Providing Custom-Made Analysis

In the third stage of development the system can move toward an even greater responsiveness to individual users' needs. In addition to providing repetitive reports for classes of users, the system should be capable of providing single-purpose, on-request analyses for classes of, or even individual, users. At this stage, the system's staffing would have to include strong analysis and marketing sections, in addition to the traditional data collection and storage. The analysts would be available to service any user in programing and running any specific requirements. Users will, again, have the choice of requesting print-outs or tapes, and they may order these as a one-time analysis or on a specified frequency basis. Note that, unlike the "idealized" system, outsiders do *not* have direct access to the data base. The only authorized access is through the system's own staff. This makes for considerably easier protection of the stored data from destruction or alteration, as well as maintenance of security and privacy. It similarly protects against equipment tie-up and scheduling problems resulting from incompetent or inefficient programing by outsiders.

As in the "idealized" system, users can be charged or shadow prices established for both analysis and data-processing services. Users who can provide the system's analysts with complete programs for their analysis will incur only the cost of checking these programs. On the other hand, a user who simply states his needs or final output, would be charged for the full cost of programing. Note, however, that the system and its staff are involved only in the data collection and analysis stages. They are not called on to make interpretations and thus are insulated from the political and other pressures inherent in that stage.

A logical first user to be given the individual analysis option could well be the federal government itself. As was clearly shown in Chapter 8, Congressional

---

*The BLS in its efforts to sell new services to new users might find the success of the Department of Agriculture's county agents in selling services to farmers instructive.

and Executive staffs would undoubtedly welcome the availability of such a service. Appropriate strengthening does not imply expertise in electronic data processing (EDP) but, rather, expertise in the *content* of their field and in structuring the information needs of particular problems. Programing and EDP skills would be provided by the system's staff. The arrangement would also permit some experimentation with pricing and charging arrangements. The service might then be extended to other federal agencies and possibly state governments through the network of USES offices.

A logical extension of the charge for services would be the development of a voucher system for some job seekers. Improving access to labor market information may entail the use of vouchers enabling low-income individuals (who, at present, may confine their dealings to USES) to avail themselves also of the services of private employment agencies. There are at least two major potential benefits of a voucher system: The first is simply an increase in the range and specificity of labor market information available to individuals and a possible reduction in discriminatory barriers; the second is the improvement in the services rendered by USES when it is subject to competition. However, there is always the possibility that a voucher system would increase the tendency of the private agencies to cream off the more easily placed applicants, leaving USES to confront an ever decreasing share of desirable job openings.

### Final Step: Toward the Ideal System

Between the third phase and the "ideal" stage lie a series of technological problems and developments. No significant change in the concepts of the service is envisioned. Rather, essentially technical problems of providing direct access under protected conditions present the key obstacles to progress.

The road we have charted is long and difficult. It represents, however, a progressive evolution with each move along this road undertaken in modest, implementable projects. An all-or-nothing attack with all its inherent dangers and demands on budgets is avoided. The rate of progress is also quite flexible, permitting it to be adjusted to the pace of successful experiences and available resources. It should also be noted that this measured progression provides the necessary time for "educating" users and permitting them to identify and develop their information needs. Users' planning and model-building, and the availability of information for these, are interdependent and self-reinforcing. Better planning calls for better information, and the availability of better information leads to better planning and model-building. Thus, progress must be paced for harmonious balance of these several components.

Finally, much experience in the development of other information systems supports the combined attack proposed here — at both the local and national levels. It provides a progressive, feasible progression toward an effective labor market information system.

## BLS MAJOR PROGRAMS, 1972

| *Programs* | *Uses* |
|---|---|

I. *Manpower and Employment*

A. *Labor Force, Employment and Unemployment*

    1. Current labor force analysis (CPS household sample)

        Over-all economic indicator; most comprehensive measure of national employment and unemployment; primary source on employment status and personal characteristics of the labor force.

    2. Urban employment survey (CPS sample)

        Measurement of economic and social conditions in these areas; provide data to program planners to pinpoint the problems of residents of poor neighborhoods in large cities.

    3. Labor force studies (CPS sample supplementary questions)

        Primary source on special aspects of labor force; used in studying factors in changing labor force participation of various population groups, such as older persons, students, and married women.

B. *Industry Employment Statistics*

    1. Employment in nonagricultural establishments (Establishment payroll reports)

        Economic indicator; mobilization and manpower planning; marketing studies; plant location planning.

    2. Hours and earnings

        Economic indicator; plant location planning; wage negotiations; adjustment of labor costs in escalator clauses of long-term contracts.

3. Job openings—labor turn-over statistics

Economic indicator; manpower planning; job market analysis; guide for State Employment Services; yardstick for individual plant performance.

C. *Occupational Employment Statistics*

1. National estimates

Evaluation of current levels of occupational employment and demand for labor by type of skill.

2. Scientific professional and technical personnel in industry and in state governments

Basis for estimating scientific and technical manpower resources, and for assessing current and future demand for scientists, engineers, and technicians—including those engaged in research and development; used by National Science Foundation and other agencies in developing national manpower policy in science and engineering.

3. Atomic Energy manpower

Provides the Atomic Energy Commission with basis for assessing changing manpower needs by occupation for atomic energy work in government-owned contractor operated, and private facilities.

4. Industry-occupational employment tables

Analysis of the occupational implications of changes in technology, output, and total employment, in industry detail for all sectors of the economy.

5. Projections of employment by occupation

Used as a tool in developing training and retraining programs, and in vocational counseling.

6. *Occupational Outlook Handbook*

Vocational guidance and counseling of high school and college students,

| | |
|---|---|
| | veterans, and other people choosing careers; personnel work; basic reference on occupational trends. |
| 7. *Occupational Outlook Quarterly* | Provides current information on developments affecting employment opportunities; supplements *Occupational Outlook Handbook* with more recent data. |

II. *Wages and Industrial Relations*

A. *Wage Studies*

| | |
|---|---|
| 1. Area surveys | Wage and salary administration; union contract negotiations; conciliation and arbitration; plant location planning; analysis of wage differentials; labor cost estimates; administrative evaluation of job offers to unemployment insurance beneficiaries. |
| 2. Industry surveys | Wage and salary administration; union contract negotiations; conciliation and arbitration; plant location planning; occupational counseling; minimum wage policy guidance; analysis of wage differentials; labor cost estimates; administrative evaluation of job offers to unemployment insurance beneficiaries. |
| 3. Professional, administrative, technical, and clerical salary surveys | Salary administration in private employment; salary structure review for Federal and other government; occupational counseling; administrative evaluation of job offers to unemployment insurance beneficiaries. |
| 4. Earnings distribution surveys | Minimum wage policy guidance: U.S. Department of Labor, the Congress, trade associations, unions, and others affected; general wage and income analysis. |

| Programs | Uses |
|---|---|
| 5. Union wage scales and hours | Union contract negotiations; arbitration proceedings; labor cost estimates; trend of union scales of wages and hours. |

B. *Compensation Studies*

| | |
|---|---|
| 1. Compensation expenditures and payroll hours | Interindustry labor expenditure comparisons; analysis of compensation in economic fluctuations; measure of trends in employer expenditures; analysis of productivity changes; international comparisons. |
| 2. Employee-benefit plans analysis of health, insurance, pensions, etc. | Collective bargaining; personnel administration; government policy-making; social welfare agencies; insurance and financial institutions; industrial relations research. |

C. *Wage Trend Studies*

| | |
|---|---|
| 1. Current wage developments | General economic analysis; public and private wage policy guidance and review; trends of changes in wages and related benefits; collective bargaining. |
| 2. Wage chronologies | Collective bargaining; historical analysis of collective bargaining; general economic analysis. |
| 3. Wage indexes | General analysis of wage trends and developments; collective bargaining; general economic analysis. |

D. *Industrial Relations Studies*

| | |
|---|---|
| Files of collective bargaining agreements, strikes and lockouts, union constitutions, etc. | Collective bargaining; arbitration and conciliation; personnel administration; government policy-making; industrial relations research; measure of strike activity; analysis of trends in collective bargaining and effect of work stoppages on econ- |

omy; industrial relations research; general information on union organization and key officials; union administration; government policy-making; industrial relations research.

III. *Productivity, Technology, and Growth*

A. *Private Economy and Sector Productivity Measurement*

    1. Trends in output per man hour and unit labor costs (private economy and sector measures)

Economic indicator; manpower requirements; studies of relationships between productivity, wages, prices, and profits; measures of economic growth and productive strength.

    2. Comparisons of outputs per man hour, labor and non-labor payments, and prices

Economic indicator; studies of relationships between costs and prices.

B. *Industry Productivity Measurement*

    Trends in output per man hours (industry measures)

Economic indicator; manpower requirements; studies of labor cost; effect of technological changes.

C. *Labor Requirements Studies*

    Construction labor requirements

Measure of labor generating effects of public works programs; assessing manpower requirements; guides to countercyclical policies; market research for construction materials.

D. *Technological Studies*

    1. Studies of technological trends in major industries

Forecasts of pace of technological change and its prospective impact; private and government policy-making; projections of economic growth.

| | |
|---|---|
| 2. Studies of major technological innovations | Forecasts of pace of technological change and its prospective impact; private and government policy-making; manpower training programs. |
| 3. Case studies of manpower adjustment to technological change | Techniques of manpower adjustments to technological change; private and government policy-making. |

E. *Economic Growth Studies*

| | |
|---|---|
| 1. Long-range projections of U.S. economic growth under assumptions of high employment. | Framework for analyzing future problems of manpower utilization; basis for developing estimates of occupational requirements by industry. |
| 2. Analytic studies of impact of economic change on employment | Major analytical tool in developing estimates of direct and indirect employment impact of changes in expenditure patterns; evaluating impact of construction programs on employment (see above.); evaluating impact of foreign trade on employment; evaluating impact of investment on employment; evaluating impact of changes in level and pattern of defense expenditures on employment in each industry. |

## Chapter 1

1. For further details, see U. S. Congress, Title I, Section 106 of the amendments to the Manpower Development and Training Act, 1968.

2. *Proceedings of a Conference on Labor Market Information Systems: Information Needs, Sources and Methods of Delivery,* Human Factors in Technology Research Group, University of California (Berkeley, November 1970), p. 64.

3. E. Wight Bakke, *A Positive Labor Market Policy* (Columbus, Ohio: Charles E. Merrill Books, 1963).

4. Ivar E. Berg and Marcia Freedman of the Conservation of Human Resources staff are conducting an analysis of "Work and Values."

## Chapter 2

1. See Charles C. Holt and M. H. David, "The Concept of Job Vacancies in a Dynamic Theory of the Labor Market," in the National Bureau of Economic Research, ed., *The Measurement and Interpretation of Job Vacancies: A Conference Report* (New York: Columbia University Press, 1966).

2. See Thomas M. Stanback, Jr., and Richard V. Knight, *The Metropolitan Economy* (New York: Columbia University Press, 1970), pp. 14-16.

3. Margaret Thal-Larsen, "Placement and Counselling in a Changing Labor Market: Public and Private Employment Agencies and Schools, 1968" (mimeo., Berkeley, University of California Institute of Industrial Relations, 1970).

4. George P. Huber and Joseph C. Ullman, "Job Bank: A Case Study of a Manpower Program." Also in progress is Malcolm S. Cohen, "Planning and Conceptualization of a Labor Market Information System."

## Chapter 3

1. "Labor Market Information and the Federal-State Employment Service System," Advisory Committee on Research to the U. S. Employment Service (Washington, D. C., February 1968).

2. *Report of the President's Committee to Appraise Employment and Unemployment Statistics: Measuring Employment and Unemployment* (Washington, D. C., 1962). This has come to be known as the "Gordon report."

3. Harold Goldstein, "The New Federal-State Occupational Employment Statistics Program," *Monthly Labor Review* (U. S. Government Bureau of Labor Statistics), October 1971, pp. 12-17.

4. *Ibid.,* p. 11.

5. Wassily W. Leontief, "Theoretical Assumptions and Non-observed Facts," *American Economic Review,* March 1971, pp. 1-17.

## Chapter 4

1. Albert Rees, "Labor Economics: Effects of More Knowledge, Information Networks in Labor Markets," Papers and Proceedings of the Seventy-ninth Annual Meeting, *American Economic Review,* LV, May 1966, pp. 559-66.

2. *Ibid.,* p. 561.

3. Thomas C. Schelling, "On the Ecology of Micromotives," *The Public Interest,* XXV, Fall 1971, p. 82.

4. Herbert S. Parnes *et al.,* the National Longitudinal Surveys. These surveys have yielded the following reports, all of which have been published by the Manpower Administration of the U. S. Department of Labor and are or will be available from the Superintendent of Documents, U. S. Government Printing Office: *The Pre-Retirement Years,* Manpower Research Monograph No. 15; *Dual Careers,* Manpower Research Monograph No. 21; *Career Thresholds,* Manpower Research Monograph No. 16; and *Years for Decision,* Manpower Research Monograph No. 24.

5. Marcia Freedman with G. Maclachlin, *The Process of Work Establishment* (New York: Columbia University Press, 1969).

6. Dale L. Hiestand, *Changing Careers After Thirty-five* (New York: Columbia University Press, 1971).

7. Gary Becker, *Human Capital* (New York: National Bureau of Economic Research, 1964).

8. For a thorough discussion of job queues, see Lester C. Thurow and Robert E. B. Lucas, *The American Distribution of Income: A Structural Problem,* U. S. Congress, Joint Economic Committee, 92nd Cong. (Washington, D. C., 1972).

9. Rhona Pavis, "Towards the Equalization of Income and Occupational Distribution of Blacks and Whites and Males and Females," Working Paper No. 113-27 (Washington, D. C.: The Urban Institute, 1969).

10. Charles Holt, "Job Search, Phillips' Wage Relation and Union Influence: Theory and Evidence," in Edmund S. Phelps *et al., Microeconomic Foundations of Employment and Inflation Theory* (New York: W. W. Norton, 1970), p. 56.

## Chapter 5

1. John T. Dunlop, "Job Vacancy Measures and Economic Analysis," in the National Bureau of Economic Research, ed., *The Measurement and Inter-*

*pretation of Job Vacancies: A Conference Report* (New York: Columbia University Press, 1966), cited in Peter B. Doeringer and Michael J. Piore, *Internal Labor Markets and Manpower Analysis* (Lexington, Mass.: D. C. Heath, 1971), pp. 1-2.

2. These findings are consistent with previous research on employer wage-gathering practices. See N. Arnold Tolles and Robert L. Raimon, *Sources of Wage Information* (Ithaca, N. Y.: Cornell University Press, 1952).

3. See William Haber and Daniel H. Kruger, *The Role of the United States Employment Service in a Changing Economy* (Kalamazoo, Mich.: The W. E. Upjohn Institute for Employment Research, 1964), pp. 70-74, 106-9; or, more recently, Stanley H. Ruttenberg and Jocelyn Gutchess, *The Federal-State Employment Service: A Critique* (Baltimore: The Johns Hopkins Press, 1970), pp. 23-27, 91-92.

4. See F. T. Malm, "Recruiting Patterns and the Functioning of Labor Markets," in F. T. Malm, Paul Pigors, and Charles A. Myers, eds., *Management of Human Resources* (New York: McGraw-Hill, 1964), pp. 242-56; and more recently, Margaret Thal-Larsen, "Changing Employer Policies in a Large Urban Labor Market," in *Proceedings of the Twenty-first Annual Winter Meeting of the Industrial Relations Research Association* (Madison, Wis.: IRRA, 1969), pp. 248-56.

5. This search procedure is analagous to that of an individual who seeks labor market information (e.g., job opportunities, wage rates) from family and friends. We are indebted to Margaret Thal-Larsen of the University of California at Berkeley for making this point more explicit in our own thinking. More generally, the discussion in this section has benefited from her helpful comments. Also see Albert Rees, "Labor Economics: Effects of More Knowledge, Information Networks in Labor Markets," Papers and Proceedings of the Seventy-ninth Annual Meeting, *American Economic Review* LV, May 1966, pp. 559-66.

6. For example, the requirement of excessive amounts of schooling (and other "qualifications") for higher-skilled manual jobs. For further discussion of this as well as other mechanisms causing informal labor market discrimination, see Walter A. Fogel, "Labor Market Obstacles to Minority Job Gains,"in *Proceedings of the Twentieth Annual Winter Meeting of the Industrial Relations Research Association* (Madison, Wis.: IRRA, 1968), pp. 97-104.

7. These concepts are discussed in Rees, "Labor Economics." Also see George J. Stigler, "Information in the Labor Market," *Journal of Political Economy,* Supplement, LXX, October 1962, pp. 94-105.

8. This concept is discussed in Wayne Vroman, "The Labor Force Reserve: A Re-Estimate," *Industrial Relations,* IX, October 1970, pp. 379-93.

9. See Michael J. Piore, "On-the-Job Training in the Dual Labor Market," in Arnold Weber *et al.,* eds., *Public-Private Manpower Policies* (Madison, Wis.: Industrial Relations Research Association, 1969), pp. 101-32.

10. See, for example, the Manpower Research Monograph series published by the U. S. Department of Labor, Manpower Administration. Twenty-three of these monographs had been issued through mid-1971.

11. The standard reference to the capital concept as applied to labor is Theodore W. Schultz's "Investment in Human Capital," *American Economic Review,* LI, March 1961, pp. 1-17. Also see "Investment in Human Beings," papers presented at a conference called by the Universities-National Bureau Committee for Economic Research, *Journal of Political Economy,* Supplement, LXX, October 1962. A contrasting view is presented in Neil W. Chamberlain, "Some Second Thoughts on the Concept of Human Capital," in *Proceedings of the Twentieth Annual Winter Meeting of the Industrial Relations Research Association (Madison, Wis.: IRRA, 1968) pp. 1-13.*

12. See R. D. Smith, "Information Systems for More Effective Use of Executive Resources," *Personnel Journal,* XLVIII, June 1969, pp. 452-58. For a more thorough examination of human asset inventories, see W. L. Brummet *et al.,* "Human Resources Accounting," *Personnel Administration,* July-August 1969, pp. 34-46.

13. Thal-Larsen, "Changing Employer Policies," p. 253.

14. This term is from John T. Dunlop. See his "Task of Contemporary Wage Theory," in George W. Taylor and Frank C. Pierson, eds., *New Concepts in Wage Determination* (New York: McGraw-Hill, 1957), pp. 117-39. For further discussion of the wage aspects of internal labor markets, see E. Robert Livernash, "The Internal Wage Structure," in Taylor and Pierson, eds., *New Concepts in Wage Determination,* pp. 140-72.

15. This distinction is made explicit by Gary Becker in his *Human Capital* (New York: National Bureau of Economic Research, 1964), pp. 8-29.

16. For an examination of the uses of schooling as a screening device in the labor market, see Ivar Berg, *Education and Jobs: The Great Training Robbery* (New York: Praeger Publishers, 1970).

17. A more complete statement of the selection process, along with a critique of the standard validation model, is presented in Marvin D. Dunnette, *Personal Selection and Placement* (Belmont, Calif.: Wadsworth Publishing, 1966), especially chs. 6-8.

18. See *Willie S. Griggs v. Duke Power Co.* (U. S. Supreme Court, No. 124, March 8, 1971).

19. See, for example, *Employer Manpower Planning and Forecasting,* U.S. Department of Labor, Manpower Administration, Manpower Research Monograph No. 19 (Washington, D. C., 1970).

20. See Dunnette, *Personnel Selection and Placement;* and Lewis E. Albright *et al., The Use of Psychological Tests in Industry* (Cleveland: Howard Allen, 1963).

21. See James Kirkpatrick *et al., Testing and Fair Employment* (New York: New York University Press, 1968); and Doris B. Rosen, *Employment Testing and Minority Groups,* Key Issues Series, No. 6 (Ithaca, N. Y.: New York State School of Industrial and Labor Relations, Cornell University, June 1970). Several of the respondents in this probe mentioned that both aptitude and personality testing needed to be further investigated. They did not, however, indicate how this might specifically affect selection processes in their own firms.

## Chapter 6

1. The material in this chapter represents a distillation of the results of an investigation of career guidance carried on by the Conservation of Human Resources over several years, which led to a recent volume by Eli Ginzberg, *Career Guidance* (New York: McGraw-Hill, 1971), particularly material found in Chapter 11, "Informational Processes: Personal Assessment," Chapter 12, "Informational Processes: The World of Work," and Part IV, "Policy." In addition, we have benefited very much from the detailed investigations carried out by Margaret Thal-Larsen and her staff at the University of California.
2. Ginzberg, *Career Guidance*, p. 167.
3. *Ibid.*
4. *Ibid.*, p. 320.
5. *Ibid.*, p. 272.
6. *Ibid.*, p. 284.

## Chapter 7

1. R. S. Eckaus, "Economic Criteria for Education and Training," *Review of Economics and Statistics,* XLIV, 1964, pp. 181-90.
2. John K. Folger and Charles B. Nam, *Education of the American Population,* 1960 Census Monograph (Washington, D. C., 1967), p. 169.
3. *Ibid.*, p. 171-72. Emphasis added.
4. *Ibid.*, p. 173.
5. *Ibid.*, p. 175.
6. *Ibid.*, p. 176.
7. For a more detailed description of the methodology, analysis, and results, see Ivar Berg, *Education and Jobs: The Great Training Robbery* (New York: Praeger Publishers, 1970), Chs. 3 and 4.
8. John K. Folger, Helen S. Astin, and Alan E. Bayer, *Human Resources and Higher Education* (New York: Russell Sage Foundation, 1970), p. 39.
9. Ann R. Miller, "Occupations of the Labor Force According to the Dictionary of Occupational Titles," (mimeo., Philadelphia, University of Pennsylvania, 1971). This report will be published as Office of Management and Budget Bulletin No. 9.
10. *Ibid.*, p. 39.
11. For a useful review, see W. Lee Hansen and David R. Witmer, "Economic Benefits of Universal Higher Education," in *Universal Higher Education: Costs and Benefits* (Washington, D. C.: American Council on Education, 1971), pp. 16-36.
12. See W. Lee Hansen and Burton A. Weisbrod, *Benefits, Costs and Finance of Public Higher Education* (Chicago: Markham Publishing, 1969).
13. Richard B. Foreman, *The Market for College Trained Manpower: A Study in the Economics of Career Choice* (Cambridge: Harvard University Press, 1971).

## Chapter 8

1. See J. E. Morton, *Analytical Potential of the Current Population Survey for Manpower and Employment Research,* Studies in Employment and Unemployment (Kalamazoo, Mich.: W. E. Upjohn Institute, 1965), p. 20.

2. *Ibid.,* p. 15.

3. *Report of the President's Committee to Appraise Employment and Unemployment Statistics: Measuring Employment and Unemployment* (Washington, D. C., 1962), passim.

4. Wassily W. Leontief, "Theoretical Assumptions and Non-observed Facts," *American Economic Review,* March 1971, p. 6.

5. *Report of the President's Committee,* passim.

6. Morton, *Analytical Potential,* pp. 31-32.

7. George P. Shultz, "The Use of Labor Statistics in National Decision-making," *Monthly Labor Review,* November 1969, p. 49.

8. *Ibid.,* p. 50.

## Chapter 9

1. Melvin Anshen, "The Federal Budget as an Instrument for Measurement and Analysis," in David Novick, ed., *Program Budgeting* (Cambridge: Harvard University Press, 1965).

2. See the evaluations by the Department of Labor of the Work Incentive (WIN) programs, summaries of which appear in the annual reports to the Congress. For an example of an attempt to achieve a tightly controlled experiment designed to yield significant relationships between income and work for lower-income groups likely to be involved in negative income tax programs, see the summary article by David N. Kershaw, "A Negative Income Tax Experiment," *Scientific American,* October 1972, pp. 19-25. For another example of a careful evaluation of an experimental program designed to dispense a particular type of job market information, see David W. Stevens, *An Experimental Labor Market Information Program to Encourage Self-Initiated Job Search by Selected Registrants with Public Employment Service Offices* (Washington, D. C.: U. S. Department of Labor, Manpower Administration, 1972).

3. J. S. Wholey *et al., Federal Evaluation Policy* (Washington, D. C.: The Urban Institute, 1970) p. 2.

4. Olympus Research Corporation, *The Total Impact Evaluation of Manpower Programs in Four Cities* (Washington, D. C.: U. S. Department of Labor Manpower Administration, Office of Evaluation, 1970).

5. Wholey *et al., Federal Evaluation Policy,* pp. 16-17.

## Chapter 10

1. Margaret Thal-Larsen, "Placement and Counselling in a Changing Labor Market: Public and Private Employment Agencies and Schools, 1968" (mimeo., Berkeley, University of California Institute of Industrial Relations, 1970).

BORIS YAVITZ is Professor of Business at the Graduate School of Business of Columbia University. He has done extensive management consultant and seminar work both in this country and abroad. He is the author of *Automation in Commercial Banking: Its Process and Impact,* co-author of *Data Processing in New York City* and has contributed chapters to several Conservation of Human Resources publications as well as to such periodicals as *The Columbia Journal of World Business.*

DEAN W. MORSE is Professor the Social Sciences at Fordham University and formerly Associate Professor of Business at the Graduate School of Business of Columbia University. He is the author of *The Peripheral Worker* and co-editor of *The Impact of Science on Technology, Technological Innovation and Society* and *The Environment of Change.*

ANNA B. DUTKA is a research economist who was for many years on the faculty of the School of General Studies, Columbia University.

All are members of the staff of the Conservation of Human Resources Project, Columbia University.

# RELATED TITLES